AUGMENTED
REALITY
DEVELOPMENT
WITH PYTHON AND OPENCV

A Step-by-Step Guide to Creating
Immersive AR Experiences

Richard D. Crowley

Table of contents

Chapter 8: Anchoring Your AR Creations: Plane Detection and Object Placement 137

Chapter 15: Fine-Tuning Your AR Creations: Optimizing AR Applications 233

Part I: Foundations

Chapter 1: Welcome to the World of Augmented Reality!

Hey there, future AR wizards! Ever wished you could see hidden layers of information in the world around you? Or maybe bring your wildest imaginations to life, right before your eyes? That's the magic of Augmented Reality (AR), and you're about to embark on an incredible journey to master it.

In this chapter, we'll break down the fundamentals of AR, explore its different forms, and discover how it's already changing the way we play, learn, work, and interact with the world. Let's dive in!

What is Augmented Reality?

Imagine this: you're walking down the street, and your phone's camera shows you not just the buildings around you, but also historical facts, reviews of nearby restaurants, or even 3D characters popping up to guide you to your destination. That's AR in action!

Beyond the Buzzword

AR is more than just a cool tech term. It's about blending the digital and physical worlds in a way that enhances your perception and interaction with your surroundings. Unlike Virtual Reality (VR), which immerses you in a completely artificial environment, AR overlays computer-generated content onto the real world, creating a mixed reality experience.

Think of it like this: VR is like stepping into a movie, while AR is like adding special effects to your everyday life.

Core Concepts

To truly grasp AR, let's break down its key ingredients:

- Digital Overlays: AR adds layers of digital information to your view of the real world. This can include anything from text and images to 3D models, animations, and even sounds. Imagine seeing virtual furniture in your living room before you buy it, or watching a 3D dinosaur roam around your backyard!
- Real-time Interaction: AR isn't just about passive viewing; it's about interacting with the digital content and your environment. You can manipulate virtual objects, trigger animations, or even play games that respond to your movements and surroundings.
- Contextual Awareness: AR systems use sensors and computer vision to understand your

environment to some extent. This allows them to place virtual objects realistically, provide relevant information based on your location, or even react to your actions in a meaningful way.

Distinguishing AR from Other Realities

It's easy to get AR confused with other immersive technologies, so let's clear things up:

- AR vs. VR: | Feature | Augmented Reality (AR) | Virtual Reality (VR) | |---|---|---| | Environment | Real world with digital overlays | Completely simulated environment | | Immersion | Partial | Full | | Hardware | Smartphones, tablets, AR glasses | VR headsets | | Typical Applications | Games, navigation, education, retail | Games, simulations, training, therapy |
- The Mixed Reality Spectrum: Mixed Reality (MR) is like AR's advanced cousin. It takes the blending of real and virtual even further, allowing digital objects to interact with the physical world more seamlessly. Imagine a virtual ball bouncing off a real table or a virtual character hiding behind a real tree!

How Augmented Reality Works

Behind the scenes, AR relies on some fascinating technology:

- The AR System Pipeline:
  - Capture: Cameras, depth sensors, and other input devices capture data about the real world, like images, depth information, and your position in space.
  - Process: Computer vision algorithms analyze the data to understand the scene, recognize objects, track your movements, and determine where to place virtual content.
  - Render: The system generates the appropriate digital content and positions it correctly in the scene.
  - Display: The augmented view is presented to you through a screen (like your phone or tablet) or a headset (like AR glasses).
- Key Technologies:
  - Computer Vision: This field of AI gives AR systems the ability to "see" and interpret the world, much like humans do. It's used for tasks like object recognition, image tracking, and scene understanding.
  - Simultaneous Localization and Mapping (SLAM): This powerful technique allows devices to map their environment and

track their position within it simultaneously. It's crucial for markerless AR, where there are no predefined markers to rely on.

○ Sensors and Hardware: AR systems rely on various sensors to gather information about the real world. These include cameras, accelerometers (to measure movement), gyroscopes (to measure orientation), GPS (for location tracking), and sometimes even depth sensors like LiDAR (to create 3D maps of the environment).

The Evolution of Augmented Reality

While AR might seem like a recent invention, its roots go way back!

- Early Visions: Pioneers like Ivan Sutherland (with his groundbreaking head-mounted display in the 1960s) and Myron Krueger (with his "artificial reality" installations in the 1970s) laid the groundwork for the AR experiences we enjoy today.
- Milestones and Breakthroughs:
  ○ Early Applications: AR first found practical applications in fields like military aviation (head-up displays in

fighter jets), manufacturing (assembly guidance), and medical training (surgical simulations).

- o The Mobile AR Revolution: The arrival of smartphones with powerful processors and cameras brought AR to the masses. Apps like Layar and Wikitude started popping up, offering early glimpses of AR's potential.
- o The Rise of AR Games: Games like Pokémon Go took the world by storm, showcasing the power of AR to engage and entertain millions of people.
- Current Trends:
  - o AR Glasses and Headsets: Companies like Microsoft (HoloLens), Magic Leap, and Apple are developing AR glasses and headsets that promise to be more comfortable, lightweight, and powerful than ever before. Imagine wearing glasses that can overlay information on your world, provide hands-free navigation, or even let you interact with virtual characters!
  - o WebAR: AR experiences are becoming more accessible thanks to WebAR, which allows you to access them directly

through your web browser, without needing to download a separate app.

Benefits and Challenges of Augmented Reality

AR has the potential to revolutionize many aspects of our lives, but it also faces some hurdles:

- Expanding Human Capabilities:
  - Enhanced Perception: AR can provide you with extra information about your surroundings, making the world more informative and engaging. Imagine seeing historical facts about landmarks as you walk by, or getting real-time translations of foreign signs.
  - Improved Communication: AR can enable new forms of communication and collaboration, allowing you to share experiences with others remotely or interact with virtual characters in a more natural way.
  - New Forms of Learning and Training: AR can create immersive and interactive learning environments, making education more engaging and effective. Imagine dissecting a virtual frog without harming any animals, or taking a virtual field trip to ancient Rome!

- Addressing the Challenges:
    - Technological Limitations: Current AR devices can be bulky, have limited battery life, and may not provide a perfectly seamless experience. But don't worry, technology is constantly improving!
    - Content Creation: Creating high-quality AR experiences requires skilled developers and designers. As the AR field grows, there's a growing demand for creative minds like yours!
    - Privacy and Ethical Concerns: As AR becomes more prevalent, it's important to address concerns about data privacy, facial recognition, and the potential for misuse. We need to ensure that AR is used responsibly and ethically.

Types of AR

Just like there are different types of cars (sports cars, SUVs, sedans), there are different types of AR, each with its own strengths and weaknesses. Let's explore the main categories:

Marker-based AR

This type of AR relies on visual markers (like QR codes or special images) to trigger the display of digital content. When your device's camera detects a marker, it calculates its position and orientation, allowing virtual objects to be placed accurately in the scene.

- How it Works:
  - Marker Detection: The AR system uses computer vision to identify and track predefined markers in the camera feed.
  - Pose Estimation: Once a marker is detected, the system figures out its position and orientation relative to the camera.
  - Content Rendering: Based on the marker's pose, the AR system renders the corresponding digital content, making it appear as if it's anchored to the marker in the real world.
- Types of Markers:
  - QR Codes: Those black-and-white squares you see everywhere can be used as AR markers. They're easy to create and can store various information.
  - Aruco Markers: These are specifically designed for AR applications and offer robust detection and tracking capabilities.
  - AprilTag Markers: Another popular choice for AR, known for their accuracy

and resistance to occlusion (being blocked from view).

- o Custom Markers: You can even create your own markers tailored to your specific AR application!

- Pros and Cons:
  - o Pros: Relatively simple to implement, accurate tracking, reliable detection.
  - o Cons: Limited flexibility (you need physical markers), markers need to be visible, markers might not always be aesthetically pleasing.
- Applications:
  - o Print media: Bring magazines, brochures, and posters to life with interactive 3D models or videos.
  - o Product visualization: Allow customers to view 3D models of products in their own homes before buying them.
  - o Games: Create interactive board games or toys that come to life with AR enhancements.
  - o Education: Develop interactive learning materials, like flashcards that turn into 3D animals or historical figures.

Markerless AR

This type of AR doesn't rely on predefined markers. Instead, it uses a combination of sensors (like GPS, accelerometers, and gyroscopes) and computer vision techniques to understand your environment and track your position. This allows virtual objects to be placed in the real world based on your location or relative to your device's position.

- Beyond Markers: Markerless AR offers more freedom and flexibility since you don't need physical markers to trigger AR experiences.
- Key Technologies:
  - SLAM: This is a crucial technology for markerless AR. It allows your device to map its surroundings and track its own position within that map, all in real-time.
  - Plane Detection: AR apps can use computer vision to detect flat surfaces like walls, floors, and tables, allowing you to place virtual objects on them realistically.
  - Location Tracking: GPS is commonly used for location-based AR experiences, but other techniques like visual-inertial odometry (VIO) can also be used to track your position and movement.
- Pros and Cons:

- Pros: Greater flexibility, seamless integration with the real world, scalability for large-scale AR experiences.
- Cons: Can be less accurate than marker-based AR, requires more processing power, performance can be affected by environmental factors (like GPS signal strength or lighting conditions).
- Applications:
  - Navigation: Get AR directions overlaid on the real world, guiding you to your destination with virtual arrows and landmarks.
  - Location-based games: Explore your city and interact with virtual creatures or objects that appear based on your location (think Pokémon Go!).
  - Tourism: Discover historical information or see virtual reconstructions of landmarks as you visit them.
  - Interior design: Place virtual furniture in your home to see how it looks before you buy it.

Projection-based AR

This type of AR uses projectors to cast light onto real-world surfaces, creating illusions of 3D objects or interactive displays. You don't need to wear any special devices to experience it, making it suitable for public installations and large-scale AR experiences.

- Light as the Medium: Projection-based AR turns ordinary surfaces into interactive canvases. Imagine a tabletop that comes to life with animated characters or a wall that transforms into a virtual window with a breathtaking view!
- Types of Projection:
  - Direct: Projecting images directly onto objects, creating illusions of 3D forms or textures.
  - Diffuse: Using scattered light for more subtle effects, like changing the appearance of a room or creating ambient lighting effects.
  - Interactive: Allowing users to interact with the projected content through touch or gestures. Imagine playing a virtual piano on a tabletop or controlling a game character with your hand movements.
- Pros and Cons:
  - Pros: Creates stunning visual effects, suitable for large-scale installations, no need for wearable devices.

- o Cons: Projection quality can be affected by ambient lighting, interactivity can be limited, equipment can be expensive.
- Applications:
  - o Art installations: Create interactive art exhibits that respond to viewers' movements or create captivating illusions.
  - o Advertising: Project interactive advertisements or information displays in public spaces.
  - o Stage performances: Enhance live performances with dynamic scenery, special effects, or interactive elements.
  - o Industrial design: Project designs onto prototypes for visualization and evaluation.

Superimposition-based AR

This type of AR replaces or modifies the appearance of real-world objects with computer-generated imagery. It's often used to enhance or alter our perception of existing objects, providing additional information or creating visual effects.

- Altering Reality: Superimposition-based AR can make objects appear different, reveal hidden details, or even replace them entirely with virtual counterparts.

- Object Recognition and Tracking: This type of AR relies heavily on computer vision to accurately identify and track objects in the real world. This ensures that the virtual content is correctly superimposed on the target object, even as it moves.
- Pros and Cons:
  - Pros: Enhances visualization, provides interactive exploration of objects, enables creative augmentation of reality.
  - Cons: Object recognition can be challenging, computationally demanding, achieving truly realistic superimposition can be difficult.
- Applications:
  - Medical imaging: Overlay X-rays or scans onto a patient's body during surgery, providing surgeons with real-time guidance.
  - Maintenance and repair: Highlight parts that need replacement or provide step-by-step instructions overlaid on the equipment itself.
  - Retail: Allow customers to virtually try on clothes, makeup, or accessories by superimposing them on their image.
  - Entertainment: Replace a person's face with a character in real-time, add special

effects to videos, or create immersive gaming experiences.

Applications of AR

AR is rapidly changing the way we live, work, and play. Let's explore some of the exciting ways AR is being used across various industries:

AR in Gaming

Get ready to level up your gaming experience! AR games bring the action into the real world, blurring the lines between the virtual and physical.

- Beyond the Screen: AR games encourage you to get up and move, explore your surroundings, and interact with virtual objects and characters in your own environment.
- Examples:
  - Pokémon Go: This global phenomenon lets you catch virtual Pokémon in real-world locations, encouraging you to explore your neighborhood and interact with other players.
  - Ingress Prime: This team-based game involves capturing "portals" at real-world

landmarks, fostering collaboration and competition among players.

- ○ Harry Potter: Wizards Unite: Step into the magical world of Harry Potter and cast spells, brew potions, and encounter fantastic beasts in your own environment.
- ○ Other AR Games: The AR gaming landscape is constantly expanding, with games like "The Walking Dead: Our World," "Jurassic World Alive," and AR experiences within existing game franchises (like "Ghostbusters World").

- Emerging Trends:
  - ○ AR Cloud Gaming: Imagine playing AR games with others in a shared, persistent virtual world, thanks to the power of cloud technology.
  - ○ AR eSports: AR is even making its way into the competitive gaming scene, with new and exciting forms of spectator experiences.

AR in Education

AR is transforming the way we learn, making education more engaging, interactive, and fun!

- Transforming Learning: AR can bring textbooks to life, visualize complex concepts, and provide hands-on learning experiences that were previously impossible.

- Examples:
  - Anatomy 4D: Explore the human body in 3D, interacting with anatomical structures and learning about their functions.
  - Google Expeditions: Take virtual field trips to historical landmarks, natural wonders, and even outer space, all from the comfort of your classroom.
  - Elements 4D: Combine virtual elements to explore chemical reactions and learn about the periodic table in a hands-on way.
  - Quiver: Bring children's coloring pages to life, allowing them to interact with their creations in AR.
  - Other Educational Apps: AR apps can teach you about anything from astronomy and history to mathematics and geography.
- Benefits:
  - Increased Engagement: AR can capture students' attention and motivate them to learn by making education more interactive and fun.

- Improved Understanding: AR can help students visualize complex concepts and grasp abstract ideas more easily.
- Hands-on Learning: AR can provide interactive simulations and virtual experiments, allowing students to learn by doing.

AR in Healthcare

AR is revolutionizing healthcare, from assisting surgeons in the operating room to helping patients with rehabilitation and disease management.

- Improving Patient Care: AR can provide healthcare professionals with real-time information, improve accuracy, and enhance patient experiences.
- Examples:
  - Surgical Navigation: AR can overlay medical images onto a patient's body during surgery, providing surgeons with precise guidance and reducing the need for invasive procedures.
  - Vein Visualization: AR can help healthcare professionals locate veins more easily for injections or blood draws, making the process less stressful for patients.

- Rehabilitation and Physical Therapy: AR games and applications can motivate patients to engage in exercises and track their progress, making rehabilitation more engaging and effective.
- Disease Management: AR apps can provide patients with interactive tools for managing chronic conditions, such as diabetes or asthma.

- Benefits:
  - Increased Accuracy: AR can improve the precision of medical procedures and reduce errors, leading to better patient outcomes.
  - Improved Patient Outcomes: AR can help patients recover faster and manage their conditions more effectively.
  - Reduced Costs: AR can help reduce healthcare costs by improving

You got it! I'll pick up right where we left off, continuing to write directly to your readers in a friendly and engaging way, and keeping all the headings formatted correctly.

AR in Industry

AR is bringing a whole new level of efficiency and innovation to the industrial world, from factory floors to construction sites.

- Boosting Productivity and Efficiency: AR can streamline workflows, improve worker training, and reduce errors in various industrial sectors.
- Examples:
  - Assembly and Manufacturing: Imagine wearing AR glasses that overlay step-by-step instructions directly onto the parts you're assembling. This can significantly reduce errors, speed up production, and improve worker training.
  - Maintenance and Repair: AR can provide technicians with real-time information and guidance while they're repairing equipment. Imagine seeing virtual diagrams overlaid on a machine, highlighting the parts that need to be fixed.
  - Remote Collaboration: AR can connect experts with technicians on-site, allowing them to collaborate remotely and solve

problems more efficiently. Imagine a technician wearing AR glasses while receiving guidance from an expert who can see the same view and provide instructions in real-time.

- ○ Design and Prototyping: AR can help designers and engineers visualize and evaluate 3D models in real-world environments. Imagine projecting a virtual model of a new car onto a real parking space to see how it looks and fits.

- Benefits:
  - ○ Increased Efficiency: AR can streamline workflows, reduce production time, and optimize resource allocation.
  - ○ Reduced Errors: AR can help prevent mistakes, improve quality control, and minimize rework.
  - ○ Improved Safety: AR can provide workers with real-time safety information, hazard warnings, and training simulations to reduce workplace accidents.

AR in Retail and E-commerce

Get ready for a shopping revolution! AR is transforming the retail experience, making it more engaging, personalized, and convenient.

- Enhancing the Shopping Experience: AR can provide customers with more information, help them make better purchase decisions, and create more interactive shopping experiences.
- Examples:
  - Virtual Try-on: Ever wished you could try on clothes without having to change in a cramped fitting room? AR apps allow you to do just that! You can virtually try on clothes, makeup, or accessories using your phone's camera.
  - Furniture Placement: See how that new sofa would look in your living room before you buy it! AR apps let you place virtual furniture in your home to see how it fits and matches your style.
  - Product Visualization: AR can provide you with interactive 3D views of products, allowing you to explore their features and details in a more engaging way.
  - Interactive Shopping Experiences: AR can create fun and interactive shopping experiences, like virtual scavenger hunts in stores or interactive product displays

that come to life when you point your phone at them.

- Benefits:
  - Increased Customer Engagement: AR can capture customers' attention and make shopping more interactive and fun.
  - Improved Purchase Decisions: AR can help customers make more informed purchase decisions by providing them with realistic product visualizations and virtual try-on experiences.
  - Increased Sales: AR can lead to increased sales by providing customers with a more engaging and personalized shopping experience.

AR in Navigation and Wayfinding

Say goodbye to getting lost! AR is making navigation more intuitive and informative, whether you're exploring a new city or navigating a complex indoor environment.

- Beyond Traditional Maps: AR can provide you with more than just a static map. It can overlay directions, points of interest, and other helpful information directly onto your view of the real world.
- Examples:

- Indoor Navigation: AR can guide you through complex indoor environments like airports, shopping malls, or hospitals. Imagine arrows and directions appearing on the floor in front of you, leading you to your gate or your favorite store.
- Outdoor Navigation: AR can enhance GPS navigation with visual cues and points of interest overlaid on your real-world view. Imagine seeing virtual landmarks or historical information pop up as you walk around a city.
- Tourist Guides: AR apps can provide you with interactive tours and information about historical landmarks, making your travels more engaging and informative.
- Benefits:
  - Improved Orientation: AR can help you orient yourself in unfamiliar environments and find your way around more easily.
  - Reduced Stress: AR can make navigation less stressful and more efficient, especially in complex or crowded places.
  - Enhanced Exploration: AR can encourage you to explore your surroundings and discover new places by providing you with real-time information and guidance.

The Future of AR

The future of AR is incredibly exciting! As technology continues to advance, we can expect even more immersive, seamless, and transformative AR experiences.

Emerging Technologies and Trends

- AR Glasses and Wearables: AR glasses and headsets are becoming more lightweight, comfortable, and powerful. Imagine wearing stylish glasses that can overlay information on your world, provide hands-free communication, or even let you interact with virtual characters in a natural way.
- Artificial Intelligence (AI): AI will play a crucial role in making AR experiences more intelligent and personalized. Imagine AR systems that can understand your preferences, anticipate your needs, and provide you with tailored information and recommendations.
- 5G and Connectivity: Faster and more reliable connectivity will enable more complex and data-intensive AR applications. Imagine seamless AR experiences that stream high-quality 3D content and allow for real-time interaction with others in a shared virtual world.

- AR Cloud: The AR Cloud is a concept of a shared, persistent AR space where users can interact with each other and virtual content in real-time. Imagine leaving virtual messages for friends in specific locations or collaborating on a virtual project in a shared AR environment.
- Spatial Computing: This emerging field combines AR, VR, and AI to create a more immersive and interconnected digital world. Imagine a world where digital information is seamlessly integrated with your physical surroundings, and you can interact with both real and virtual objects in a natural and intuitive way.

Potential Impacts of AR

AR has the potential to transform many aspects of our lives, from the way we work and learn to the way we communicate and entertain ourselves.

- Work and Productivity: AR could revolutionize the workplace, enabling remote collaboration, hands-free access to information, and more efficient training. Imagine collaborating with colleagues in a shared AR environment, even if you're miles apart.
- Social Interaction and Communication: AR could change the way we communicate and interact with each other, creating new forms of social

experiences and virtual communities. Imagine attending a virtual concert with friends from around the world or sharing AR experiences with loved ones in real-time.

- Entertainment and Media: AR could revolutionize entertainment, creating immersive and interactive experiences that blur the lines between reality and fiction. Imagine watching movies where characters step out of the screen and interact with your living room, or playing games where the virtual world seamlessly blends with your real surroundings.
- Education and Learning: AR could transform education, making learning more engaging, personalized, and accessible. Imagine exploring historical events through immersive AR reconstructions or learning new skills through interactive AR simulations.
- Healthcare and Medicine: AR could revolutionize healthcare, enabling more accurate diagnoses, less invasive treatments, and more effective patient care. Imagine surgeons using AR to visualize organs in 3D during surgery or patients using AR apps to manage their chronic conditions more effectively.

Ethical Considerations

As AR becomes more prevalent, it's important to consider the ethical implications and ensure that this powerful technology is used responsibly.

- Privacy and Data Security: AR applications often collect personal data, such as your location, facial features, and even your eye movements. It's crucial to protect this data and ensure that it's used ethically and responsibly.
- Misinformation and Manipulation: AR could be used to spread misinformation or manipulate users' perceptions. We need to be critical of the information we see in AR and develop strategies to combat misinformation and ensure that AR is used for good.
- Accessibility and Inclusivity: AR experiences should be designed to be accessible to everyone, including people with disabilities. We need to ensure that AR technology is inclusive and doesn't create new barriers to participation.
- Social and Cultural Impact: AR could have a profound impact on social norms, cultural values, and human behavior. We need to be mindful of these potential impacts and ensure that AR is used to promote positive social and cultural change.

Code Challenge: Your First AR Application

Ready to get your hands dirty with some code? Let's create a simple marker-based AR application that displays a 3D model on top of a detected marker.

Objective: Create an AR app that displays a 3D model (like a cube or a character) on top of a detected marker.

Tools: We'll use OpenCV (a powerful computer vision library) and Aruco markers (easy-to-use AR markers).

Steps:

1. Marker Detection: Use OpenCV to detect the marker from your device's camera feed.
2. Pose Estimation: Calculate the marker's position and orientation in 3D space.
3. 3D Model Loading: Load a simple 3D model (you can find free models online).
4. Rendering: Render the 3D model on top of the marker, aligning it with the marker's pose so it appears anchored to the marker in the real world.

This simple challenge will introduce you to the core concepts of marker-based AR and give you a taste of what it's like to build your own AR applications. We'll provide you with detailed instructions and code examples in the following chapters, so don't worry if you're new to coding.

Congratulations! You've completed the first chapter and gained a solid understanding of what AR is, its different types, its applications, and its exciting future. Now, let's move on to the next chapter and start building your own AR experiences!

Chapter 2: Setting Up Your AR Workshop

Alright, eager AR developers! Now that you've got a grasp of the AR landscape, it's time to roll up our sleeves and set up your very own AR development environment. Think of this as building your workshop, where you'll craft amazing AR experiences.

In this chapter, we'll guide you through installing the essential software tools, introduce you to powerful Python libraries, and help you configure your camera and hardware. By the end, you'll have everything you need to start coding your first AR applications. Let's get started!

Installing Python and OpenCV

Python is our language of choice for AR development – it's versatile, beginner-friendly, and has a fantastic ecosystem of libraries for computer vision and AR. OpenCV (Open Source Computer Vision Library) is our trusty sidekick, providing the tools to process images, detect objects, and understand the world through your camera.

Why Python for AR?

Python's clear syntax and readability make it a joy to work with, even for coding newcomers. Plus, it boasts a rich collection of libraries that simplify complex tasks, allowing you to focus on the creative aspects of AR development.

Why OpenCV for AR?

OpenCV is the go-to library for computer vision tasks. It's packed with functions for image processing, object detection, camera calibration, and more. It's like a Swiss Army knife for AR developers!

Installing Python

1. Download Python: Head over to the official Python website (python.org) and download the latest version for your operating system (Windows, macOS, or Linux).
2. Run the Installer: Follow the on-screen instructions to install Python. Make sure to check the box that adds Python to your system's PATH environment variable. This allows you to run Python commands from your terminal or command prompt.

Installing OpenCV

1. Using pip: Open your terminal or command prompt and type the following command:
2. Bash

```
pip install opencv-python
```

3.
4. This will install the OpenCV library using pip, Python's package installer.
5. Verify Installation: Open a Python interpreter (by typing python in your terminal) and try importing OpenCV:
6. Python

```
import cv2

print(cv2.__version__)
```

7.
8. If this prints the OpenCV version without any errors, you're good to go!

Essential Python Libraries for AR

Besides OpenCV, there are a few other Python libraries that will come in handy for AR development. Think of them as specialized tools in your AR workshop.

NumPy

NumPy is the foundation for numerical computing in Python. It provides powerful array objects and tools for working with them. In AR, we'll use NumPy for tasks like:

- Image Representation: Images are essentially arrays of pixels, and NumPy provides efficient ways to store and manipulate them.
- Mathematical Operations: NumPy makes it easy to perform mathematical operations on image data, such as matrix transformations or calculations for 3D geometry.

To install NumPy, use pip:

Bash

```
pip install numpy
```

SciPy

SciPy builds on NumPy and provides additional tools for scientific computing. We'll use SciPy for tasks like:

- Image Filtering: SciPy offers various image filtering functions that can be used to smooth images, sharpen edges, or remove noise.
- Linear Algebra: SciPy provides tools for linear algebra operations, which are essential for tasks like 3D transformations and camera calibration.

To install SciPy, use pip:

Bash

```
pip install scipy
```

Matplotlib

Matplotlib is a popular library for creating visualizations in Python. We'll use Matplotlib for tasks like:

- Displaying Images: Matplotlib provides functions for displaying images and videos, which is helpful for visualizing the output of our AR algorithms.
- Plotting Data: Matplotlib can be used to create plots and graphs, which can be useful for

analyzing data or visualizing the performance of our AR applications.

To install Matplotlib, use pip:

Bash

pip install matplotlib

Introduction to IDEs

An Integrated Development Environment (IDE) is like your AR workbench – it provides a comfortable and efficient environment for writing, testing, and debugging your code.

PyCharm

PyCharm is a popular IDE specifically designed for Python development. It offers features like:

- Intelligent Code Completion: PyCharm suggests code as you type, helping you write code faster and with fewer errors.
- Debugging Tools: PyCharm provides powerful debugging tools that help you find and fix errors in your code.

- Code Navigation: PyCharm makes it easy to navigate through your code, jump to definitions, and find usages of variables and functions.

You can download PyCharm from the JetBrains website (jetbrains.com/pycharm).

VS Code

VS Code (Visual Studio Code) is a lightweight and versatile code editor that has excellent support for Python. It offers features like:

- Extensions: VS Code has a vast library of extensions that add support for various languages and frameworks, including Python and OpenCV.
- Integrated Terminal: VS Code has a built-in terminal, which is convenient for running Python commands and scripts.
- Customization: VS Code is highly customizable, allowing you to personalize your coding environment to your preferences.

You can download VS Code from the official website (code.visualstudio.com).

Choosing an IDE

Both PyCharm and VS Code are excellent choices for AR development. Ultimately, the best IDE for you depends on your personal preferences and coding style. Experiment with both and see which one you prefer.

Configuring Your Camera and Hardware

To bring your AR creations to life, you'll need a camera to capture the real world. Most laptops and smartphones have built-in cameras, but you can also use external webcams or specialized AR headsets.

Accessing Your Camera with OpenCV

OpenCV makes it easy to access your camera and capture video frames. Here's a simple Python script to test your camera:

```python
Python

import cv2


 Open the default camera
cap = cv2.VideoCapture(0)


 Check if the camera opened successfully
```

```python
if not cap.isOpened():
    print("Error opening video stream or file")
    exit()


Continuously capture frames
while(True):
    Capture frame-by-frame
    ret, frame = cap.read()


    Display the resulting frame
    cv2.imshow('Frame', frame)


    Break the loop when 'q' is pressed
    if cv2.waitKey(1) & 0xFF == ord('q'):
        break


When everything done, release the capture
cap.release()
cv2.destroyAllWindows()
```

This script opens your default camera, captures frames, and displays them in a window. Press 'q' to exit.

Troubleshooting Camera Issues

If you encounter any issues accessing your camera, here are some troubleshooting tips:

- Check Camera Connections: Make sure your camera is properly connected to your computer.
- Update Drivers: Ensure your camera drivers are up to date.
- Camera Permissions: Check if your operating system or browser has granted permission for your Python script to access the camera.

Code Challenge: Camera Calibration

Camera calibration is an important step in AR development. It helps you correct for distortions in your camera's lens, ensuring that virtual objects are placed accurately in the real world.

Objective: Calibrate your camera using OpenCV and save the calibration parameters.

Tools: OpenCV, a checkerboard pattern (you can print one or find one online).

Steps:

1. Capture Images: Take multiple pictures of the checkerboard pattern from different angles and distances.

2. Detect Corners: Use OpenCV's findChessboardCorners function to detect the corners of the checkerboard in each image.

3. Calibrate Camera: Use OpenCV's calibrateCamera function to calculate the camera's intrinsic and extrinsic parameters.

4. Save Parameters: Save the calibration parameters to a file so you can use them in your AR applications.

This challenge will introduce you to the camera calibration process and provide you with valuable skills for creating accurate AR experiences.

Congratulations! You've successfully set up your AR development environment, installed the essential tools, and configured your camera. Now you're ready to dive into the exciting world of AR coding! Let's move on to the next chapter and start building your first AR applications.

Part II: Computer Vision Fundamentals for AR

Chapter 3: Becoming an Image Sorcerer with OpenCV

Get ready to unlock the secrets of image manipulation! In this chapter, we'll dive into the heart of computer vision with OpenCV, learning how to load, display, transform, and analyze images. Think of this as learning the spells and incantations of an image sorcerer, preparing you to work wonders in your AR applications.

Loading and Displaying Images

Before we can cast any image spells, we need to learn how to summon images into our Python realm. OpenCV makes this a breeze!

Reading Images with OpenCV

OpenCV's imread() function is your magic wand for loading images. Here's the incantation:

Python

```
import cv2
```

Load an image named "my_image.jpg"

```
image = cv2.imread("my_image.jpg")
```

This simple spell reads the image from your computer and stores it in the image variable. OpenCV supports various image formats, including JPG, PNG, TIFF, and more.

Displaying Images with OpenCV

Now that you've summoned an image, let's reveal it to the world using OpenCV's imshow() function:

Python

Display the image in a window titled "My Image"

```
cv2.imshow("My Image", image)
```

Wait for a key press

```
cv2.waitKey(0)
```

Close all windows

```
cv2.destroyAllWindows()
```

This spell opens a window titled "My Image" and displays your image. The cv2.waitKey(0) line pauses the execution until you press any key, giving you time to admire your handiwork. Finally, cv2.destroyAllWindows() closes the window.

Understanding Image Representation

Under the hood, OpenCV represents images as NumPy arrays. This means that each pixel in the image is stored as a numerical value in a multi-dimensional array. This representation allows us to perform mathematical operations on images and apply various image processing techniques.

Working with Color Images

Color images are typically represented using the BGR (Blue-Green-Red) color space in OpenCV. This means that each pixel is represented by three values: one for blue, one for green, and one for red. You can access individual color channels or convert the image to other color spaces (like grayscale or HSV) for specific image processing tasks.

Example: Loading and Displaying a Color Image

Python

```
import cv2

Load a color image

image = cv2.imread("colorful_scene.jpg")

Display the color image

cv2.imshow("Color Image", image)

cv2.waitKey(0)

cv2.destroyAllWindows()

Convert the image to grayscale

gray_image = cv2.cvtColor(image, cv2.COLOR_BGR2GRAY)

Display the grayscale image

cv2.imshow("Grayscale Image", gray_image)

cv2.waitKey(0)

cv2.destroyAllWindows()
```

This example demonstrates how to load a color image, display it, and then convert it to grayscale before displaying it again.

Image Filtering and Transformations

Now that you can summon and reveal images, let's learn how to transform and enhance them with OpenCV's image filtering spells.

Image Filtering

Image filtering is like applying magical potions to your images, altering their appearance and enhancing specific features. OpenCV provides a wide range of filters for various purposes.

- Blurring: Blurring filters, like Gaussian blur or median blur, can be used to reduce noise in images or smooth out fine details.
- Sharpening: Sharpening filters enhance edges and details in images, making them appear crisper.
- Edge Detection: Edge detection filters, like the Canny edge detector, highlight the boundaries between objects in an image.

Image Transformations

Image transformations allow you to manipulate the geometry of an image, like resizing, rotating, or warping it.

- Resizing: You can resize images to make them larger or smaller, which is useful for adapting images to different screen sizes or resolutions.
- Rotation: You can rotate images by a specified angle, which can be useful for correcting image orientation or creating special effects.
- Affine Transformations: Affine transformations allow you to perform more complex geometric transformations, like shearing, scaling, and translating images.

Example: Applying a Gaussian Blur

Python

```
import cv2

Load an image

image = cv2.imread("noisy_image.jpg")

Apply a Gaussian blur with a kernel size of 5x5

blurred_image = cv2.GaussianBlur(image, (5, 5), 0)


Display the original and blurred images

cv2.imshow("Original Image", image)

cv2.imshow("Blurred Image", blurred_image)
```

```
cv2.waitKey(0)

cv2.destroyAllWindows()
```

This example demonstrates how to apply a Gaussian blur to an image to reduce noise.

Example: Resizing and Rotating an Image

Python

```
import cv2


Load an image
image = cv2.imread("my_image.jpg")


Resize the image to half its original size
resized_image = cv2.resize(image, None, fx=0.5, fy=0.5)
Rotate the image by 45 degrees
rows, cols = image.shape[:2]
M = cv2.getRotationMatrix2D((cols/2, rows/2), 45, 1)
rotated_image = cv2.warpAffine(image, M, (cols, rows))
```

Display the resized and rotated images

```
cv2.imshow("Resized Image", resized_image)

cv2.imshow("Rotated Image", rotated_image)

cv2.waitKey(0)

cv2.destroyAllWindows()
```

This example shows how to resize an image and rotate it by a specified angle.

Color Spaces and Thresholding

Color spaces and thresholding are powerful tools for analyzing and segmenting images. They allow you to isolate specific objects or regions of interest based on their color or intensity.

Color Spaces

Color spaces are different ways of representing colors numerically. OpenCV supports various color spaces, including:

- BGR: The default color space in OpenCV, where each pixel is represented by blue, green, and red values.

- Grayscale: A single-channel representation where each pixel is represented by its intensity (brightness).
- HSV: The Hue-Saturation-Value color space, which is often more intuitive for humans to understand and manipulate.

Thresholding

Thresholding is a technique for converting a grayscale image into a binary image (black and white) by setting a threshold value. Pixels with intensity values above the threshold are set to white, while those below are set to black. This can be useful for isolating objects or regions of interest based on their intensity.

Example: Converting to HSV and Thresholding

Python

```
import cv2

Load an image
image = cv2.imread("colorful_objects.jpg")


Convert the image to HSV color space
hsv_image = cv2.cvtColor(image, cv2.COLOR_BGR2HSV)
```

Define lower and upper bounds for a specific color (e.g., red)

lower_red = (0, 100, 100)

upper_red = (10, 255, 255)

Create a mask for the red color

mask = cv2.inRange(hsv_image, lower_red, upper_red)

Apply the mask to the original image

result = cv2.bitwise_and(image, image, mask=mask)

Display the original image, mask, and result

cv2.imshow("Original Image", image)

cv2.imshow("Mask", mask)

cv2.imshow("Result", result)

cv2.waitKey(0)

cv2.destroyAllWindows()

This example demonstrates how to convert an image to HSV color space, create a mask for a specific color range (red in this case), and use the mask to isolate the red objects in the image.

Feature Detection and Matching

Feature detection and matching are essential techniques for many computer vision tasks, including object recognition, image stitching, and 3D reconstruction. These techniques allow us to identify and track specific points or patterns in images, even if the images are distorted or viewed from different angles.

Feature Detection

Feature detection algorithms identify distinctive points or patterns in an image, such as corners, edges, or blobs. These features are typically invariant to scale, rotation, and illumination changes, making them robust for various applications.

Feature Matching

Once features are detected in two or more images, feature matching algorithms find correspondences between them. This allows us to establish relationships between different views of the same scene or object.

SIFT, SURF, and ORB

OpenCV provides several feature detection and matching algorithms, including:

- SIFT (Scale-Invariant Feature Transform): SIFT is a highly robust algorithm that detects and describes local features in images. It's invariant to scale, rotation, and illumination changes, but it can be computationally expensive.
- SURF (Speeded-Up Robust Features): SURF is a faster alternative to SIFT that provides similar performance.
- ORB (Oriented FAST and Rotated BRIEF): ORB is a fast and efficient algorithm that is suitable for real-time applications. It's not as robust as SIFT or SURF, but it's a good choice when speed is a priority.

Example: Feature Matching with ORB

```python
Python

import cv2


Load two images
image1 = cv2.imread("image1.jpg")
```

```
image2 = cv2.imread("image2.jpg")

Convert images to grayscale

gray1 = cv2.cvtColor(image1, cv2.COLOR_BGR2GRAY)

gray2 = cv2.cvtColor(image2, cv2.COLOR_BGR2GRAY)

Initialize ORB detector

orb = cv2.ORB_create()

Find the keypoints and descriptors with ORB

keypoints1, descriptors1 = orb.detectAndCompute(gray1, None)

keypoints2, descriptors2 = orb.detectAndCompute(gray2, None)

Create a BFMatcher object

bf           =           cv2.BFMatcher(cv2.NORM_HAMMING,
crossCheck=True)


Match descriptors

matches = bf.match(descriptors1, descriptors2)


Sort them in the order of their distance

matches = sorted(matches, key=lambda x: x.distance)

Draw first 10 matches
```

```
matched_image = cv2.drawMatches(image1, keypoints1,
image2, keypoints2, matches[:10], None,
flags=cv2.DrawMatchesFlags_NOT_DRAW_SINGLE_POINTS
)
```

Display the matched image

```
cv2.imshow("Matched Image", matched_image)

cv2.waitKey(0)

cv2.destroyAllWindows()
```

This example demonstrates how to use ORB to detect and match features in two images. It then draws lines connecting the matched features, visualizing the correspondences between the images.

Code Challenge: Image Mosaic

Image mosaicing is a technique for combining multiple images to create a wider view of a scene. It's a common application of feature detection and matching.

Objective: Create an image mosaic from two overlapping images.

Tools: OpenCV, two overlapping images.

Steps:

1. Feature Detection and Matching: Detect and match features between the two images using a suitable algorithm (e.g., ORB).
2. Homography Estimation: Estimate the homography matrix that relates the two images using the matched features.
3. Image Warping: Warp one of the images to align it with the other image using the homography matrix.
4. Image Blending: Blend the two warped images together to create the final mosaic.

This challenge will allow you to apply your knowledge of feature detection and matching to a practical application and create a visually impressive result

Congratulations! You've now mastered the basics of image processing with OpenCV. You can load, display, transform, and analyze images, preparing you for the exciting AR challenges ahead. Let's continue our journey and explore the world of marker-based AR in the next chapter!

Chapter 4: Tapping into the Power of Live Video

It's time to bring your AR creations to life with the magic of live video! In this chapter, we'll learn how to access your camera feed with OpenCV, process video streams in real-time, and extract meaningful information from the dynamic world around you. This is where your AR applications start to truly interact with their environment.

Accessing Camera Feeds with OpenCV

OpenCV provides a simple yet powerful way to tap into your camera's video stream. It's like opening a portal to the real world, allowing your AR applications to see and respond to their surroundings.

VideoCapture: Your Gateway to Live Video

The `cv2.VideoCapture` class is your key to accessing camera feeds. It acts as a bridge between your code and your camera, allowing you to capture frames, control camera settings, and even work with video files.

Here's the basic incantation to open your default camera:

Python

```
import cv2
```

Open the default camera (usually with index 0)

```
cap = cv2.VideoCapture(0)
```

Check if the camera opened successfully

```
if not cap.isOpened():
    print("Error opening video stream or file")
    exit()
```

This code snippet creates a VideoCapture object (cap) that represents your camera. The 0 usually refers to your default camera. If you have multiple cameras, you can try other indices (1, 2, etc.) to access them.

Capturing Frames

Once you have a VideoCapture object, you can capture frames from the video stream using the read() method:

Python

Capture frame-by-frame

```
ret, frame = cap.read()
```

This line reads a single frame from the camera and stores it in the frame variable. The ret variable is a boolean value that indicates whether the frame was captured successfully.

Displaying the Video Feed

To display the live video feed, we can use a loop that continuously captures and displays frames:

Python

```
while(True):
    Capture frame-by-frame
    ret, frame = cap.read()


    Display the resulting frame
    cv2.imshow('Live Video', frame)


    Break the loop when 'q' is pressed
```

```python
if cv2.waitKey(1) & 0xFF == ord('q'):
    break
```

When everything done, release the capture

```python
cap.release()

cv2.destroyAllWindows()
```

This code snippet captures frames in a loop and displays them in a window titled "Live Video". The cv2.waitKey(1) function allows you to control the frame rate and also provides a way to exit the loop by pressing the 'q' key. Finally, cap.release() releases the camera and cv2.destroyAllWindows() closes all windows.

Working with Video Files

You can also use VideoCapture to work with video files. Simply provide the path to the video file instead of the camera index:

Python

```python
cap = cv2.VideoCapture("my_video.mp4")
```

This will open the video file "my_video.mp4" and allow you to process it frame by frame.

Video Processing Techniques

Now that you can access live video, let's explore some common video processing techniques that are essential for AR development.

Frame Differencing

Frame differencing is a simple yet effective technique for detecting motion in a video. It involves comparing consecutive frames and identifying the pixels that have changed. This can be used to detect moving objects or track changes in the scene.

```python
Python

import cv2


 Open the default camera
cap = cv2.VideoCapture(0)


 Read the first frame
ret, previous_frame = cap.read()
```

```
previous_frame_gray          =          cv2.cvtColor(previous_frame,
cv2.COLOR_BGR2GRAY)

while(True):

    Capture frame-by-frame

    ret, frame = cap.read()

    gray = cv2.cvtColor(frame, cv2.COLOR_BGR2GRAY)


    Calculate the absolute difference between the current frame
and the previous frame

    frame_diff = cv2.absdiff(gray, previous_frame_gray)


    Threshold the difference image to highlight moving pixels

        _,   thresh   =   cv2.threshold(frame_diff,   30,   255,
cv2.THRESH_BINARY)


    Display the resulting frame

    cv2.imshow('Frame Difference', thresh)

    Update the previous frame

    previous_frame_gray = gray


    Break the loop when 'q' is pressed
```

```
if cv2.waitKey(1) & 0xFF == ord('q'):

    break
```

When everything done, release the capture

```
cap.release()

cv2.destroyAllWindows()
```

This code snippet demonstrates how to perform frame differencing and highlight moving pixels in a video stream.

Optical Flow

Optical flow is a more sophisticated technique for motion analysis. It estimates the motion of pixels between consecutive frames, providing information about the direction and speed of movement. This can be used for tasks like object tracking, motion estimation, and video stabilization.

OpenCV provides several optical flow algorithms, including Lucas-Kanade and Farneback.

Color Tracking

Color tracking allows you to track objects in a video based on their color. This can be useful for isolating specific objects or regions of interest in a dynamic scene.

You can use color spaces like HSV to define color ranges and then use thresholding techniques to create masks that isolate the desired colors.

Background Subtraction and Object Detection

Background subtraction is a powerful technique for isolating moving objects from a static background. It involves creating a model of the background and then subtracting it from each frame to identify the foreground objects.

OpenCV provides several background subtraction algorithms, including:

- MOG2: A Gaussian Mixture-based Background/Foreground Segmentation Algorithm.
- KNN: K-Nearest Neighbors based Background/Foreground Segmentation Algorithm.

Once you have isolated the foreground objects, you can apply object detection techniques to identify and track them.

Object Detection with OpenCV

OpenCV provides several object detection methods, including:

- Haar Cascades: A machine learning-based approach for detecting objects with predefined features (like faces, eyes, or cars).
- HOG + SVM: Histogram of Oriented Gradients (HOG) features combined with a Support Vector Machine (SVM) classifier for object detection.
- Deep Learning-based Object Detection: Using pre-trained deep learning models (like YOLO or SSD) for more accurate and robust object detection.

Camera Calibration and Distortion Correction

Camera calibration is a crucial step in AR development. It allows you to correct for distortions introduced by your camera's lens, ensuring that virtual objects are placed accurately in the real world.

Understanding Distortion

Most cameras introduce some degree of distortion, especially wide-angle lenses. This can cause straight lines to appear curved or objects to appear distorted in shape.

- Radial Distortion: Causes straight lines to curve outwards (barrel distortion) or inwards (pincushion distortion).
- Tangential Distortion: Occurs when the camera's lens is not perfectly parallel to the image sensor.

Calibration Process

Camera calibration involves taking multiple images of a known pattern (like a checkerboard) from different angles and distances. OpenCV provides functions to detect the corners of the pattern in each image and then estimate the camera's intrinsic and extrinsic parameters.

- Intrinsic Parameters: Describe the internal characteristics of the camera, such as focal length, principal point, and distortion coefficients.
- Extrinsic Parameters: Describe the camera's position and orientation in the world.

Distortion Correction

Once you have the camera's parameters, you can use OpenCV's undistort() function to correct for distortion in images or video frames. This ensures that your AR applications perceive the real world accurately.

Code Challenge: Real-time Object Tracking

Object tracking is a common application of video processing techniques. It involves identifying and following an object in a video stream.

Objective: Implement a real-time object tracking system using OpenCV.

Tools: OpenCV, a camera.

Steps:

1. Object Detection: Use a suitable object detection method (e.g., color tracking, Haar cascades) to detect the object in the first frame.
2. Object Tracking: Use an object tracking algorithm (e.g., MeanShift, CAMShift) to track the object in subsequent frames.
3. Visualization: Draw a bounding box around the tracked object in each frame.

This challenge will allow you to apply your knowledge of video processing and object detection to create a dynamic AR application that can interact with moving objects in the real world.

Congratulations! You've now learned how to work with cameras and video using OpenCV. You can access camera feeds, apply video processing techniques, perform background subtraction and object detection, and even calibrate your camera to correct for distortion. You're well on your way to becoming an AR master!

Part III: Marker-Based Augmented Reality

Chapter 5: Unleashing the Power of Markers: Detection and Tracking

Prepare to enter the realm of marker-based AR, where digital content springs to life from special codes and patterns! In this chapter, we'll delve into the fascinating world of AR markers, learn how to detect and track them with OpenCV, and unlock the secrets of pose estimation and 3D tracking.

By the end, you'll be able to conjure virtual objects that seem to magically appear from real-world markers, creating immersive and interactive AR experiences. Let's begin our marker-based adventure!

Understanding AR Markers

AR markers are like secret codes that unlock digital content in the real world. They act as anchors, allowing your AR applications to precisely place and track virtual objects in relation to these markers. Think of them as doorways between the physical and digital realms.

What Makes a Good AR Marker?

Not all images or patterns make good AR markers. Ideal markers have a few key characteristics:

- High Contrast: Markers should have clear, sharp edges and high contrast between black and white regions. This makes them easily detectable by computer vision algorithms, even in varying lighting conditions.
- Unique Features: Each marker should have a unique pattern or code that distinguishes it from others. This allows your AR application to identify specific markers and trigger the corresponding digital content.
- Fast Detection: Markers should be designed for fast and efficient detection. This ensures smooth and responsive AR experiences, even on resource-constrained devices.

Types of AR Markers

There are several popular types of AR markers, each with its own strengths and weaknesses:

- Aruco Markers: These are widely used markers that are specifically designed for AR applications. They are robust, easy to generate, and provide accurate pose estimation. OpenCV provides excellent support for Aruco markers.

- AprilTag Markers: These markers are known for their high accuracy and robustness to occlusion (being partially hidden from view). They are a good choice for applications that require precise tracking.
- QR Codes: While primarily used for encoding data, QR codes can also be used as AR markers. They are easily recognizable and widely available, but they may not be as robust as Aruco or AprilTag markers for AR tracking.

Aruco Markers in Depth

Aruco markers are a popular choice for AR development due to their robustness and ease of use. They consist of a black border and an inner binary matrix that encodes a unique identifier.

- Aruco Dictionaries: OpenCV provides several predefined Aruco dictionaries, each containing a set of unique markers. You can choose a dictionary based on the number of markers you need and the desired marker size.
- Marker Generation: OpenCV allows you to easily generate Aruco markers with your chosen dictionary and identifier. You can then print these markers or display them on a screen to use in your AR applications.
- Advantages:

- Robust Detection: Aruco markers are designed to be detected reliably even under challenging lighting conditions or partial occlusion.
- Accurate Pose Estimation: The four corners of the marker provide enough information for accurate pose estimation, allowing you to determine the marker's position and orientation in 3D space.
- Error Detection and Correction: The binary encoding of Aruco markers allows for error detection and correction, improving the reliability of marker detection.

AprilTag Markers in Depth

AprilTag markers are another excellent choice for AR applications, especially those that require high accuracy and robustness.

- Structure and Encoding: AprilTag markers have a more complex structure than Aruco markers, with a larger variety of patterns and a higher information density.
- Advantages:
  - High Accuracy: AprilTag markers provide very accurate pose estimation,

making them suitable for applications that require precise tracking.

- o Robustness to Occlusion: AprilTag markers are designed to be detected even when partially occluded, making them more reliable in real-world scenarios.
- o Open Source: AprilTag is an open-source library, providing flexibility and customization options.

Marker Detection with OpenCV

OpenCV makes it incredibly easy to detect AR markers in images or video streams. It's like having a magical lens that can instantly recognize these special codes.

Aruco Marker Detection

Here's the basic incantation for detecting Aruco markers with OpenCV:

```python
Python

import cv2


Load the predefined dictionary
```

```
aruco_dict                                        =
cv2.aruco.Dictionary_get(cv2.aruco.DICT_6X6_250)
```

Initialize the detector parameters

```
aruco_params = cv2.aruco.DetectorParameters_create()
```

Load an image or capture a frame from the camera

```
image = cv2.imread("image_with_markers.jpg")
```

Detect the markers in the image

```
(corners, ids, rejected) = cv2.aruco.detectMarkers(image,
aruco_dict, parameters=aruco_params)
```

This code snippet loads a predefined Aruco dictionary, initializes the detector parameters, and then uses the cv2.aruco.detectMarkers() function to detect markers in the image.

- corners: A list of detected marker corners. Each corner is represented by a list of four coordinates (x, y).
- ids: A list of identifiers for the detected markers.
- rejected: A list of potential markers that were rejected during the detection process.

AprilTag Marker Detection

Detecting AprilTag markers with OpenCV requires using the apriltag library. Here's a basic example:

Python

```python
import cv2
from apriltag import apriltag

 Initialize the AprilTag detector
detector = apriltag("tag36h11")

 Load an image or capture a frame from the camera
image = cv2.imread("image_with_apriltags.jpg")
gray = cv2.cvtColor(image, cv2.COLOR_BGR2GRAY)

 Detect the AprilTags in the image
results = detector.detect(gray)


 Print the results
for r in results:
    print(r)
```

This code snippet initializes an AprilTag detector, loads an image, and then uses the detector.detect() function to detect AprilTags in the image. The results variable contains information about the detected tags, such as their IDs, corners, and pose.

Pose Estimation and 3D Tracking

Once you've detected an AR marker, the next step is to estimate its pose, which means determining its position and orientation in 3D space. This is crucial for accurately placing and tracking virtual objects in your AR applications.

How Pose Estimation Works

Pose estimation involves using the detected marker corners and the camera's intrinsic parameters (focal length, principal point) to calculate the marker's pose relative to the camera. This is typically done using a technique called Perspective-n-Point (PnP).

OpenCV provides the cv2.solvePnP() function to perform pose estimation. This function takes the marker corners, the camera's intrinsic parameters, and the distortion coefficients as input and outputs the rotation and translation vectors that describe the marker's pose.

3D Tracking

3D tracking involves continuously estimating the pose of the marker as it moves in the scene. This allows you to keep virtual objects anchored to the marker, even as the camera or the marker moves around.

You can achieve 3D tracking by detecting the marker in each frame of a video stream and then estimating its pose. This creates a dynamic AR experience where virtual objects seem to be attached to the real-world marker.

Example: Aruco Marker Pose Estimation

```python
Python

import cv2

import numpy as np


Load the predefined dictionary

aruco_dict                                              =
cv2.aruco.Dictionary_get(cv2.aruco.DICT_6X6_250)


Initialize the detector parameters

aruco_params = cv2.aruco.DetectorParameters_create()
```

Load the camera calibration parameters

```
camera_matrix = np.load("camera_matrix.npy")

dist_coeffs = np.load("dist_coeffs.npy")
```

Load an image or capture a frame from the camera

```
image = cv2.imread("image_with_markers.jpg")
```

Detect the markers in the image

```
(corners, ids, rejected) = cv2.aruco.detectMarkers(image, aruco_dict, parameters=aruco_params)


if ids is not None:
```

Estimate the pose of the detected markers

```
        rvecs, tvecs, _ = cv2.aruco.estimatePoseSingleMarkers(corners, 0.05, camera_matrix, dist_coeffs)
```

Draw the axes on the image

```
    for i in range(len(ids)):

        cv2.aruco.drawAxis(image, camera_matrix, dist_coeffs, rvecs[i], tvecs[i], 0.1)
```

Display the resulting image

```
cv2.imshow("Pose Estimation", image)

cv2.waitKey(0)

cv2.destroyAllWindows()
```

This example demonstrates how to detect Aruco markers in an image, estimate their pose, and then draw 3D axes on the markers to visualize their orientation in space.

Handling Marker Occlusion and Loss

In real-world AR scenarios, markers may be partially or completely occluded (hidden from view) or even lost temporarily. Robust AR applications need to handle these situations gracefully to provide a seamless experience.

Occlusion Handling

When a marker is partially occluded, the marker detection algorithm may still be able to detect it, but the pose estimation may be less accurate. To handle this, you can use techniques like:

- Error Detection and Correction: Aruco markers have built-in error detection and correction capabilities that can help improve tracking even with partial occlusion.

- Predictive Tracking: If the marker is temporarily occluded, you can use predictive tracking algorithms to estimate its position based on its previous trajectory.
- Robust Pose Estimation: Use robust pose estimation algorithms that can handle missing or noisy data.

Marker Loss

If a marker is completely lost, your AR application needs to recover gracefully. You can use techniques like:

- Re-detection: Continuously attempt to re-detect the marker in the video stream.
- Visual Feedback: Provide visual feedback to the user, indicating that the marker is lost and guiding them to bring it back into view.
- Switching to Markerless Tracking: If the marker is lost for an extended period, you could potentially switch to markerless tracking techniques to maintain the AR experience.

Example: Handling Marker Loss with Re-detection

Python

```
import cv2

... (Aruco marker detection and pose estimation code) ...


while(True):

    Capture frame-by-frame
    ret, frame = cap.read()


    Detect the markers in the image
        (corners, ids, rejected) = cv2.aruco.detectMarkers(frame,
    aruco_dict, parameters=aruco_params)


    if ids is not None:
        Estimate the pose of the detected markers

                                    rvecs,     tvecs,    _     _
    cv2.aruco.estimatePoseSingleMarkers(corners,           0.05,
    camera_matrix, dist_coeffs)


        ... (render virtual objects on the markers) ...
    else:

        Marker is lost, display a message
```

```
        cv2.putText(frame, "Marker Lost!", (100, 100),
cv2.FONT_HERSHEY_SIMPLEX, 1, (0, 0, 255), 2)


    Display the resulting frame

    cv2.imshow("Marker Tracking", frame)


    Break the loop when 'q' is pressed

    if cv2.waitKey(1) & 0xFF == ord('q'):

        break


... (release the camera and destroy windows) ...
```

This example demonstrates how to handle marker loss by displaying a message to the user when the marker is not detected. You could extend this to include re-detection logic or switch to markerless tracking.

Code Challenge: Interactive AR Cube

Let's combine your knowledge of marker detection, pose estimation, and 3D rendering to create an interactive AR experience!

Objective: Create an AR application that displays a 3D cube on top of an Aruco marker. Allow the user to rotate the cube by rotating the marker.

Tools: OpenCV, Aruco markers, a 3D cube model (you can create one or find one online).

Steps:

1. Marker Detection and Pose Estimation: Detect an Aruco marker in the video stream and estimate its pose.
2. 3D Cube Rendering: Render a 3D cube model on top of the marker, aligning it with the marker's pose.
3. Rotation Control: Use the marker's rotation to control the rotation of the 3D cube.

This challenge will allow you to create a truly interactive AR experience where the virtual object responds to the user's actions in the real world.

Congratulations! You've now mastered the fundamentals of marker detection and tracking with OpenCV. You can detect markers, estimate their pose, track them in 3D space, and even handle occlusion and marker loss. You're well-equipped to create engaging and robust marker-based AR applications. Let's continue our AR journey and explore the world of markerless AR in the next chapter!

Chapter 6: Breathing Life into Your AR World with 3D Objects

Get ready to transform your AR experiences from flat overlays to immersive 3D worlds! In this chapter, we'll dive into the exciting realm of 3D graphics, learn how to render 3D models with OpenCV, and master the art of seamlessly blending virtual objects with the real world.

By the end, you'll be able to conjure realistic 3D objects that appear to inhabit the physical world, creating truly captivating and interactive AR experiences. Let's embark on this 3D adventure!

Introduction to 3D Graphics

Before we start conjuring 3D objects, let's take a moment to understand the fundamental building blocks of 3D graphics. Think of these as the essential ingredients for creating your virtual masterpieces.

Meshes: The Shape of Things

Meshes are the foundation of 3D models. They define the shape and structure of objects using a network of interconnected vertices (points), edges (lines connecting vertices), and faces (polygons formed by edges).

Imagine a mesh as a digital sculpture, where vertices are like the clay, edges are the wires holding it together, and faces are the surfaces that define its form.

- Types of Meshes: There are various types of meshes, each with its own characteristics and applications:
    - Triangle Meshes: The most common type, where faces are triangles. They are simple, efficient, and widely supported by graphics hardware.
    - Quad Meshes: Meshes where faces are quadrilaterals (four-sided polygons). They can provide smoother surfaces than triangle meshes.
    - Polygon Meshes: Meshes where faces can have any number of sides. They offer more flexibility but can be more complex to work with.

Textures: Dressing Up Your Models

Textures are like the skin of your 3D models. They add color, detail, and realism to the surfaces of your objects. Imagine textures as images that are wrapped around your meshes, giving them the appearance of different materials like wood, metal, or fabric.

- Types of Textures: There are various types of textures, each serving a different purpose:
  - Diffuse Textures: Define the base color and pattern of a surface.
  - Normal Maps: Create the illusion of surface detail by altering the way light reflects off the surface.
  - Specular Maps: Control how shiny or reflective a surface appears.

Lighting: Bringing Your Scene to Life

Lighting is essential for creating realistic and immersive 3D scenes. It simulates the way light interacts with objects, creating shadows, highlights, and reflections that give your virtual world depth and dimension.

- Types of Lights: There are various types of lights in 3D graphics:
  - Ambient Light: Provides overall illumination to the scene.
  - Directional Light: Simulates light coming from a specific direction, like the sun.
  - Point Light: Emits light from a single point in all directions, like a light bulb.
  - Spot Light: Emits light in a cone-shaped beam, like a spotlight.

3D Coordinate Systems

3D graphics use coordinate systems to define the position and orientation of objects in space. The most common coordinate system is the Cartesian coordinate system, which uses three axes (X, Y, and Z) to represent points in 3D space.

- Transformations: You can manipulate 3D objects using transformations like translation (moving), rotation (turning), and scaling (resizing). These transformations are essential for positioning and animating your virtual objects in the AR scene.

Rendering 3D Models with OpenCV

While OpenCV is primarily a computer vision library, it also provides some basic functionality for rendering 3D objects. This allows you to integrate 3D models into your AR applications without relying on external 3D graphics libraries.

Rendering with solvePnP and projectPoints

OpenCV's solvePnP() function, which we used for pose estimation in the previous chapter, can also be used for rendering 3D models. By providing the 3D coordinates of the object's vertices and the camera's pose, solvePnP()

calculates the 2D projection of those vertices onto the image plane.

You can then use OpenCV's projectPoints() function to project the 3D points onto the image, taking into account the camera's intrinsic parameters and distortion coefficients.

Limitations of OpenCV for 3D Rendering

OpenCV's 3D rendering capabilities are limited compared to dedicated 3D graphics libraries like OpenGL or DirectX. It doesn't support advanced features like lighting, textures, or complex shaders. However, it's a good starting point for simple 3D rendering tasks in AR applications.

Example: Rendering a 3D Cube

```python
Python

import cv2

import numpy as np


 Load the camera calibration parameters
camera_matrix = np.load("camera_matrix.npy")
```

```python
dist_coeffs = np.load("dist_coeffs.npy")
```

Define the 3D coordinates of the cube's vertices

```python
cube_vertices = np.float32([[-1, -1, -1], [-1, -1, 1], [-1, 1, 1], [-1, 1, -1],

                            [1, -1, -1], [1, -1, 1], [1, 1, 1], [1, 1, -1]])
```

Define the edges of the cube

```python
cube_edges = [(0, 1), (1, 2), (2, 3), (3, 0),

              (4, 5), (5, 6), (6, 7), (7, 4),

              (0, 4), (1, 5), (2, 6), (3, 7)]
```

Load an image or capture a frame from the camera

```python
image = cv2.imread("image.jpg")
```

... (Aruco marker detection and pose estimation code) ...

```python
if ids is not None:
```

Project the 3D points onto the image

```
    imgpts,  _  =  cv2.projectPoints(cube_vertices,  rvecs[0],
tvecs[0], camera_matrix, dist_coeffs)


  Draw the cube edges on the image

  imgpts = np.int32(imgpts).reshape(-1, 2)

  for i, j in cube_edges:

        cv2.line(image, tuple(imgpts[i]), tuple(imgpts[j]), (0, 255,
0), 3)


  Display the resulting image

cv2.imshow("3D Cube Rendering", image)

cv2.waitKey(0)

cv2.destroyAllWindows()
```

This example demonstrates how to render a 3D cube on top of an Aruco marker. It defines the 3D coordinates of the cube's vertices, projects them onto the image using the marker's pose, and then draws the cube edges on the image.

Aligning Virtual Objects with Markers

The key to creating convincing AR experiences is to seamlessly align virtual objects with the real-world markers. This involves accurately placing the 3D model in the scene and ensuring that it moves and rotates in sync with the marker.

Using the Marker's Pose

The marker's pose, which we estimated using solvePnP(), provides the crucial information for aligning virtual objects. The rotation and translation vectors describe the marker's position and orientation in 3D space.

By applying the same rotation and translation to the 3D model, you can ensure that it's perfectly aligned with the marker in the AR scene.

Scaling the 3D Model

You may also need to scale the 3D model to match the size of the marker in the real world. This can be done by multiplying the model's vertices by a scaling factor.

Example: Aligning a 3D Model with a Marker

Python

... (Aruco marker detection and pose estimation code) ...

```
if ids is not None:

    Get the rotation and translation vectors
    rvec, tvec = rvecs[0], tvecs[0]


    Define the scaling factor
    scale_factor = 0.1


    Scale the 3D model
    scaled_vertices = cube_vertices scale_factor


    Project the scaled 3D points onto the image
    imgpts, _ = cv2.projectPoints(scaled_vertices, rvec, tvec,
camera_matrix, dist_coeffs)


    ... (draw the 3D model on the image) ...
```

This example demonstrates how to scale a 3D model and align it with an Aruco marker using the marker's pose.

Interactive AR Applications with Markers

Marker-based AR opens up a world of possibilities for creating interactive experiences. By combining marker detection, pose estimation, and 3D rendering, you can build AR applications that respond to user actions and dynamically change the virtual scene.

User Input and Interaction

You can use various methods to capture user input in your AR applications:

- Mouse Clicks: Detect mouse clicks on the AR display to trigger actions or select virtual objects.
- Keyboard Input: Use keyboard keys to control virtual objects or navigate the AR scene.
- Touch Input: For touch-enabled devices, capture touch events to interact with virtual objects or trigger actions.

Dynamic Content and Animations

You can create dynamic AR experiences by changing the appearance or behavior of virtual objects based on user input or real-world events. This can involve:

- Animations: Animate virtual objects to create movement and life in your AR scene.

- Interactive Elements: Allow users to manipulate virtual objects, trigger animations, or change the appearance of the scene.
- Real-world Triggers: Use real-world events, like marker movement or object detection, to trigger changes in the virtual scene.

Example: Interactive Cube Rotation

Python

... (Aruco marker detection and pose estimation code) ...

```
if ids is not None:

    Get the rotation vector

    rvec = rvecs[0]


    Allow the user to rotate the cube using the 'a' and 'd' keys

    if cv2.waitKey(1) & 0xFF == ord('a'):

        rvec[0][0] += 0.1   Rotate around the X-axis

    if cv2.waitKey(1) & 0xFF == ord('d'):

        rvec[0][0] -= 0.1   Rotate around the X-axis
```

Project the 3D points onto the image using the updated rotation

imgpts, _ = cv2.projectPoints(scaled_vertices, rvec, tvec, camera_matrix, dist_coeffs)

... (draw the 3D model on the image) ...

This example demonstrates how to allow the user to interactively rotate a 3D cube in an AR scene by pressing the 'a' and 'd' keys.

Code Challenge: AR Treasure Hunt

Let's create an engaging AR treasure hunt game using marker-based AR!

Objective: Create an AR application that hides a virtual treasure chest behind an Aruco marker. Guide the user to find the treasure chest by displaying directional arrows on other markers.

Tools: OpenCV, Aruco markers, a 3D treasure chest model, arrow images.

Steps:

1. Marker Setup: Create several Aruco markers. One marker will hide the treasure chest, while others will display directional arrows.
2. Marker Detection and Pose Estimation: Detect all markers in the video stream and estimate their poses.
3. Treasure Chest Rendering: Render the 3D treasure chest model on top of the designated marker.
4. Directional Arrows: Display arrow images on the other markers, pointing towards the treasure chest.
5. Game Logic: When the user points their camera at the treasure chest marker, display a "You found the treasure!" message.

This challenge will allow you to create an interactive AR game that combines marker detection, pose estimation, 3D rendering, and game logic.

Congratulations! You've now learned how to augment reality with 3D objects. You can render 3D models with OpenCV, align them with markers, and create interactive AR experiences. You're well on your way to becoming an AR wizard!

Part IV: Markerless Augmented Reality

Chapter 7: Venturing into Markerless AR: Feature Tracking and SLAM

Prepare to break free from the constraints of markers and enter the dynamic world of markerless Augmented Reality! In this chapter, we'll explore the fascinating techniques of feature tracking and Simultaneous Localization and Mapping (SLAM), which allow your AR applications to understand and navigate the world without relying on predefined markers.

By the end, you'll be able to create AR experiences that seamlessly blend virtual content with the environment, even as the camera moves freely through the scene. Let's embark on this markerless adventure!

Feature Tracking Algorithms

Feature tracking is like giving your AR application a set of eyes that can follow points of interest in the environment. It involves identifying distinctive features in images and tracking their movement over time, providing valuable information about the scene's dynamics and the camera's motion.

What are Features?

Features are distinctive points or patterns in an image that can be easily identified and tracked. They are typically corners, edges, or blobs that stand out from their surroundings. Good features are:

- Repeatable: They can be reliably detected in different images of the same scene, even under varying lighting or viewpoints.
- Distinctive: They are unique enough to be distinguished from other features in the image.
- Local: They are localized to a small region of the image, making them less susceptible to occlusion.

Optical Flow

Optical flow is a technique for estimating the motion of pixels between consecutive frames in a video. It analyzes how pixel intensities change over time to determine the direction and speed of movement.

- Applications: Optical flow has various applications in computer vision, including:
  - Motion Estimation: Determining the movement of objects or the camera in a scene.
  - Video Stabilization: Removing camera shake or jitter from videos.

- Object Tracking: Following the movement of objects in a video stream.
- OpenCV Implementation: OpenCV provides several optical flow algorithms, including:
  - Lucas-Kanade: A classic algorithm that tracks features using a sparse approach.
  - Farneback: A dense optical flow algorithm that estimates motion for every pixel in the image.

KLT (Kanade-Lucas-Tomasi) Tracker

The KLT tracker is a popular feature tracking algorithm that combines the Lucas-Kanade optical flow method with a feature selection strategy. It identifies good features to track (corners with high contrast) and then uses optical flow to estimate their motion between frames.

- Advantages:
  - Efficiency: KLT is relatively fast and efficient, making it suitable for real-time applications.
  - Accuracy: It provides accurate tracking for well-defined features.
- OpenCV Implementation: OpenCV provides the cv2.goodFeaturesToTrack() function to find good features to track and the

cv2.calcOpticalFlowPyrLK() function to track those features using the Lucas-Kanade method.

Example: Feature Tracking with KLT

Python

```python
import cv2
import numpy as np


 Open the default camera
cap = cv2.VideoCapture(0)


 Parameters for ShiTomasi corner detection
feature_params = dict( maxCorners = 100,
                qualityLevel = 0.3,
                minDistance = 7,
                blockSize = 7 )


 Parameters for Lucas Kanade optical flow
lk_params = dict( winSize  = (15,15),
                maxLevel = 2,
```

```
            criteria = (cv2.TERM_CRITERIA_EPS |
cv2.TERM_CRITERIA_COUNT, 10, 0.03))
```

Create some random colors

```
color = np.random.randint(0,255,(100,3))
```

Take first frame and find corners in it

```
ret, old_frame = cap.read()

old_gray = cv2.cvtColor(old_frame, cv2.COLOR_BGR2GRAY)

p0 = cv2.goodFeaturesToTrack(old_gray, mask = None,
feature_params)
```

Create a mask image for drawing purposes

```
mask = np.zeros_like(old_frame)
```

```
while(1):

    ret,frame = cap.read()

                    frame_gray    =    cv2.cvtColor(frame,
cv2.COLOR_BGR2GRAY)
```

Calculate optical flow

```
p1, st, err = cv2.calcOpticalFlowPyrLK(old_gray, frame_gray,
p0, None, lk_params)


Select good points
good_new = p1[st==1]
good_old = p0[st==1]


Draw the tracks
for i,(new,old) in enumerate(zip(good_new,good_old)):
    a,b = new.ravel()
    c,d = old.ravel()
    mask = cv2.line(mask, (a,b),(c,d), color[i].tolist(), 2)
    frame = cv2.circle(frame,(a,b),5,color[i].tolist(),-1)


img = cv2.add(frame,mask)


cv2.imshow('frame',img)
k = cv2.waitKey(30) & 0xff
if k == 27:
    break
```

Now update the previous frame and previous points

```
old_gray = frame_gray.copy()
p0 = good_new.reshape(-1,1,2)


cv2.destroyAllWindows()
cap.release()
```

This example demonstrates how to use the KLT tracker to track features in a live video stream. It detects good features to track in the first frame and then uses optical flow to estimate their motion in subsequent frames. The tracked features are visualized by drawing lines connecting their positions in consecutive frames.

Introduction to Simultaneous Localization and Mapping (SLAM)

SLAM is a powerful technique that allows robots and devices to map their environment and track their own location within that map simultaneously. It's like exploring a new city while drawing a map of it at the same time.

The Chicken-and-Egg Problem

SLAM addresses a classic chicken-and-egg problem:

- To accurately map the environment, you need to know your location.
- To accurately determine your location, you need a map of the environment.

SLAM algorithms solve this problem by iteratively refining both the map and the device's location estimate.

Key Components of SLAM

- Mapping: Creating a representation of the environment, typically using landmarks (distinctive features or objects) or occupancy grids (representing free and occupied space).
- Localization: Estimating the device's position and orientation within the map.
- Data Association: Matching sensor measurements (like camera images or lidar scans) to existing landmarks or map features.
- Loop Closure: Recognizing previously visited locations to correct for accumulated errors in the map and location estimate.

Types of SLAM

- Visual SLAM: Uses cameras to map the environment and track the device's location.
- Lidar SLAM: Uses lidar sensors to create 3D maps of the environment.
- Sensor Fusion SLAM: Combines data from multiple sensors (like cameras, lidar, and inertial measurement units) to improve accuracy and robustness.

Applications of SLAM

SLAM has numerous applications in robotics and AR, including:

- Robot Navigation: Enabling robots to autonomously navigate in unknown environments.
- Augmented Reality: Creating AR experiences that seamlessly blend virtual content with the real world, even as the user moves around.
- 3D Reconstruction: Building 3D models of environments from sensor data.
- Autonomous Driving: Helping self-driving cars perceive and navigate their surroundings.

Building a Simple SLAM System with OpenCV

While building a full-fledged SLAM system is a complex task, OpenCV provides some basic tools and functionalities that allow you to create a simple SLAM system for educational purposes or experimentation.

Key Steps

1. Feature Detection and Tracking: Use a feature tracking algorithm (like KLT) to track features in the video stream.
2. Pose Estimation: Estimate the camera's pose (position and orientation) from the tracked features using techniques like Perspective-n-Point (PnP).
3. Map Building: Create a map of the environment by triangulating the positions of the tracked features.
4. Loop Closure: (Optional) Implement a loop closure algorithm to recognize previously visited locations and correct for accumulated errors.

OpenCV Tools

- Feature Tracking: cv2.goodFeaturesToTrack(), cv2.calcOpticalFlowPyrLK()
- Pose Estimation: cv2.solvePnP()
- Triangulation: cv2.triangulatePoints()

Example: Simple Visual SLAM

Python

```python
import cv2
import numpy as np


... (Feature tracking with KLT code from previous section) ...


Initialize an empty list to store the 3D points
points_3d = []


Initialize the camera pose
pose = np.eye(4)


while(1):
    ... (Capture frame, detect and track features) ...


    if len(good_new) > 8:
        Estimate the camera pose
```

```python
        _, rvec, tvec, inliers =
cv2.solvePnPRansac(np.array(points_3d), good_new,
camera_matrix, dist_coeffs)


    Update the camera pose
    R, _ = cv2.Rodrigues(rvec)
    pose[:3, :3] = R
    pose[:3, 3] = tvec.flatten()


    Triangulate new points
    if len(points_3d) == 0:
        points_3d = cv2.triangulatePoints(np.eye(3, 4), pose[:3,
:4], good_old, good_new)
        points_3d /= points_3d[3]
    else:
        new_points_3d = cv2.triangulatePoints(np.eye(3, 4),
pose[:3, :4], good_old, good_new)
        new_points_3d /= new_points_3d[3]
        points_3d = np.concatenate((points_3d, new_points_3d),
axis=1)


    ... (Visualize the map and camera trajectory) ...
```

... (Update previous frame and points) ...

This example demonstrates a simplified visual SLAM implementation. It tracks features, estimates the camera pose, and triangulates the 3D positions of the tracked features to build a map. You can extend this example to include more advanced features like loop closure and map optimization.

Code Challenge: SLAM-based AR Navigation

Let's combine your knowledge of SLAM and AR to create a navigation application!

Objective: Create an AR application that uses SLAM to map the environment and guide the user to a specific location.

Tools: OpenCV, a camera.

Steps:

1. SLAM Implementation: Implement a simple visual SLAM system using OpenCV.

2. Target Location: Define a target location in the map.
3. Navigation Guidance: Overlay directional arrows or a path on the video feed, guiding the user towards the target location.
4. Real-time Updates: Update the navigation guidance in real-time as the user moves through the environment.

This challenge will allow you to create a practical AR application that leverages SLAM for navigation and guidance.

Congratulations! You've now explored the world of feature-based tracking and SLAM. You can track features in video streams, understand the principles of SLAM, and even build a simple SLAM system with OpenCV. You're well-equipped to create markerless AR experiences that seamlessly blend virtual content with the dynamic real world. Let's continue our AR journey and explore more advanced techniques in the next chapter!

Chapter 8: Anchoring Your AR Creations: Plane Detection and Object Placement

Prepare to seamlessly integrate your AR creations with the real world! In this chapter, we'll explore the powerful technique of plane detection, which allows your AR applications to identify flat surfaces in the environment and accurately place virtual objects on them.

By the end, you'll be able to create AR experiences where virtual objects appear to rest on tables, floors, and walls, as if they truly belong in the physical world. Let's dive into the world of plane detection and object placement!

Detecting Planes and Surfaces in the Real World

Plane detection is like giving your AR application the ability to "see" flat surfaces in the environment. It involves analyzing camera images or depth data to identify planar regions, such as tables, floors, walls, and other flat objects.

Why Plane Detection Matters

Plane detection is crucial for creating realistic and immersive AR experiences. It allows you to:

- Accurately Place Objects: By identifying planes, you can precisely position virtual objects on them, making them appear as if they are resting on real-world surfaces.
- Enable Environmental Interaction: Plane detection enables virtual objects to interact with the environment, such as bouncing off walls or sliding across tables.
- Enhance Realism: Accurately placing objects on detected planes significantly enhances the realism of your AR experiences, making virtual content blend seamlessly with the real world.

How Plane Detection Works

Plane detection algorithms typically analyze depth data or camera images to identify planar regions. Here's a simplified overview of the process:

1. Depth Estimation: If using depth data (from sensors like LiDAR or stereo cameras), the algorithm analyzes the depth values to identify regions with similar depths, which may indicate a plane.

2. Feature Extraction: If using camera images, the algorithm extracts features like edges and corners, which can be used to identify potential planar regions.
3. Plane Fitting: The algorithm fits a mathematical model (usually a plane equation) to the identified regions, estimating the plane's parameters (orientation and position).
4. Plane Validation: The algorithm validates the detected planes based on criteria like size, orientation, and confidence level.

Plane Detection with OpenCV

While OpenCV doesn't have built-in plane detection functionalities, you can use external libraries or frameworks to perform plane detection and then integrate the results with your OpenCV-based AR applications.

- ARKit and ARCore: These popular AR frameworks provide robust plane detection capabilities for iOS and Android devices, respectively. You can use their APIs to detect planes and obtain their parameters.
- PCL (Point Cloud Library): If you're working with depth data, PCL provides powerful tools for point cloud processing and plane detection.

Example: Integrating ARKit Plane Detection

Python

This is a conceptual example, as specific implementation details depend on ARKit integration

```python
import cv2


... (ARKit initialization and plane detection code) ...


while True:
    ... (ARKit frame capture and plane retrieval) ...


    for plane in detected_planes:
        Get the plane's parameters (e.g., center, extent, orientation)
        plane_center = plane.center

        plane_extent = plane.extent

        plane_transform = plane.transform


        ... (Use OpenCV to draw the plane or place virtual objects
using the plane's parameters) ...
```

... (Display the AR scene) ...

This example demonstrates how you might integrate
ARKit's plane detection capabilities with your
OpenCV-based AR application. You would use ARKit's
APIs to detect planes and obtain their parameters, which
you can then use in your OpenCV code to visualize the
planes or place virtual objects on them.

Placing Virtual Objects on Planes

Once you've detected planes in the environment, the next
step is to accurately place virtual objects on them. This
involves transforming the 3D model of your virtual
object to align it with the detected plane's position and
orientation.

Transformation and Alignment

To place a virtual object on a plane, you need to apply a
transformation that aligns the object's coordinate system
with the plane's coordinate system. This typically
involves:

1. Translation: Moving the object to the plane's
   center.

2. Rotation: Rotating the object to match the plane's orientation.
3. Scaling: (Optional) Scaling the object to fit the plane's size or to achieve the desired visual effect.

Coordinate Systems and Transformations

Understanding coordinate systems and transformations is crucial for accurately placing virtual objects. Here's a brief overview:

- World Coordinate System: The global coordinate system of your AR scene.
- Plane Coordinate System: The local coordinate system of the detected plane.
- Object Coordinate System: The local coordinate system of the virtual object.

You need to transform the object's coordinates from its local coordinate system to the world coordinate system, taking into account the plane's position and orientation.

Example: Placing a Cube on a Detected Plane

Python

... (Plane detection code) ...

```
for plane in detected_planes:

    ... (Get plane parameters) ...


    Define the 3D coordinates of the cube

    cube_vertices = np.float32([[-1, -1, -1], [-1, -1, 1], [-1, 1, 1],
[-1, 1, -1],

                      [1, -1, -1], [1, -1, 1], [1, 1, 1], [1, 1, -1]])


    Define the scaling factor

    scale_factor = 0.1


    Scale the cube

    scaled_vertices = cube_vertices scale_factor


    Create a transformation matrix that aligns the cube with the
plane

    transform_matrix = np.eye(4)

    transform_matrix[:3, :3] = plane_transform[:3, :3]   Rotation

    transform_matrix[:3, 3] = plane_center   Translation
```

Apply the transformation to the cube vertices

```
transformed_vertices =
cv2.transform(np.array([scaled_vertices]), transform_matrix)[0]
```

Project the transformed vertices onto the image

```
imgpts, _ = cv2.projectPoints(transformed_vertices, rvec, tvec,
camera_matrix, dist_coeffs)
```

... (Draw the cube on the image) ...

This example demonstrates how to place a 3D cube on a detected plane. It creates a transformation matrix that aligns the cube with the plane's position and orientation and then applies this transformation to the cube's vertices before projecting them onto the image.

Environmental Interaction and Physics

To create truly immersive AR experiences, virtual objects should not only be placed accurately in the environment but also interact with it realistically. This involves simulating physical interactions like collisions, gravity, and friction.

Collision Detection

Collision detection algorithms determine whether two or more objects are intersecting in space. This is crucial for preventing virtual objects from passing through real-world surfaces or each other.

- Bounding Boxes: A simple approach is to use bounding boxes (rectangular boxes that enclose objects) to detect collisions.
- More Advanced Techniques: For more complex shapes, you can use techniques like ray casting or mesh-based collision detection.

Physics Simulation

Physics engines simulate the behavior of objects in the real world, taking into account forces like gravity, friction, and collisions. This allows you to create realistic interactions between virtual objects and the environment.

- Gravity: Simulate the effect of gravity on virtual objects, making them fall realistically.
- Friction: Simulate friction between virtual objects and surfaces, affecting their movement and sliding behavior.
- Collisions: Resolve collisions between virtual objects and real-world surfaces or other virtual objects.

Integrating Physics Engines

You can integrate physics engines like Bullet or PhysX with your AR applications to simulate realistic physics interactions. These engines provide functionalities for collision detection, rigid body dynamics, and constraint solving.

Example: Simulating a Bouncing Ball

Python

This is a conceptual example, as specific implementation details depend on the physics engine used

```
import cv2
```

... (Plane detection code) ...

Initialize the physics engine

```
physics_engine = PhysicsEngine()
```

Create a sphere object in the physics engine

```
sphere = physics_engine.create_sphere(radius=0.1, mass=1.0)
```

```
while True:

    ... (Capture frame and detect planes) ...


    Update the sphere's position based on physics simulation
    physics_engine.step_simulation()
    sphere_position = sphere.get_position()


    Project the sphere's position onto the image
        imgpts, _ = cv2.projectPoints(np.array([sphere_position]),
rvec, tvec, camera_matrix, dist_coeffs)


    ... (Draw the sphere on the image) ...


    Check for collisions with planes
    for plane in detected_planes:
        if physics_engine.check_collision(sphere, plane):
            Handle the collision (e.g., bounce the sphere)
            sphere.apply_impulse(bounce_direction, bounce_force)
```

... (Display the AR scene) ...

This example demonstrates how you might integrate a physics engine to simulate a bouncing ball in your AR application. The physics engine updates the ball's position based on gravity and collisions with the detected planes.

Code Challenge: AR Physics Playground

Let's create an interactive AR physics playground where users can interact with virtual objects and simulate realistic physics!

Objective: Create an AR application that allows users to place virtual objects (like cubes, spheres, or dominoes) on detected planes and interact with them using touch input. Simulate realistic physics interactions like collisions, gravity, and friction.

Tools: OpenCV, a physics engine (like Bullet or PhysX), a camera, touch-enabled device (optional).

Steps:

1. Plane Detection: Detect planes in the environment.

2. Object Placement: Allow users to place virtual objects on the detected planes using touch input or other interaction methods.
3. Physics Simulation: Use a physics engine to simulate realistic interactions between the virtual objects and the environment.
4. User Interaction: Allow users to interact with the virtual objects by applying forces, impulses, or constraints.

This challenge will allow you to combine your knowledge of plane detection, object placement, and physics simulation to create a fun and engaging AR experience.

Congratulations! You've now learned how to detect planes, place virtual objects on them, and simulate realistic environmental interactions. You can create AR experiences where virtual objects seamlessly blend with the real world and respond to user actions in a physically plausible way. Keep up the great work, and let's continue exploring the exciting world of AR!

Part V: Advanced AR Techniques

Chapter 9: Supercharging AR with Machine Learning

Get ready to infuse your AR applications with the power of Artificial Intelligence! In this chapter, we'll explore how to integrate machine learning (ML) with AR, enabling your creations to understand and interact with the world in intelligent ways. We'll delve into object detection and recognition using YOLO and TensorFlow, explore pose estimation with MediaPipe, and learn how to build truly AI-powered AR experiences.

By the end, you'll be able to create AR applications that can recognize objects, track human poses, and respond intelligently to the environment, opening up a whole new realm of possibilities for immersive and interactive experiences. Let's embark on this AI-powered AR journey!

Object Detection and Recognition with YOLO and TensorFlow

Object detection and recognition are like giving your AR application the ability to "see" and understand the objects in its surroundings. It involves identifying and classifying objects in images or video streams, enabling your AR creations to interact with the real world in more meaningful ways.

YOLO (You Only Look Once)

YOLO is a state-of-the-art object detection algorithm that is known for its speed and accuracy. It works by dividing the image into a grid and predicting bounding boxes and class probabilities for each grid cell.

- Advantages:
    - Real-time Performance: YOLO is incredibly fast, making it suitable for real-time AR applications.
    - High Accuracy: It achieves impressive accuracy on various object detection benchmarks.
    - Open Source: YOLO is an open-source project, providing flexibility and customization options.
- Versions: There are several versions of YOLO, with each iteration improving upon the previous one in terms of speed and accuracy. YOLOv3, YOLOv4, and YOLOv5 are some of the popular versions used today.

TensorFlow

TensorFlow is a powerful open-source machine learning framework developed by Google. It provides a comprehensive ecosystem of tools and libraries for building and deploying machine learning models,[2] including object detection models.

- TensorFlow Lite: For mobile and embedded devices, TensorFlow Lite provides a lightweight version of TensorFlow that is optimized for performance and efficiency.

Integrating YOLO with OpenCV

You can integrate YOLO with OpenCV to perform object detection in your AR applications. Here's a simplified workflow:

1. Load the YOLO Model: Load the pre-trained YOLO model (weights and configuration files) using OpenCV's dnn module.
2. Pre-process the Image: Resize and normalize the input image to match the YOLO model's requirements.
3. Inference: Pass the pre-processed image through the YOLO model to obtain the detection results (bounding boxes, class probabilities, and confidence scores).
4. Post-processing: Filter the detection results based on confidence scores and apply non-maximum

suppression to remove redundant bounding boxes.

5. Visualization: Draw the bounding boxes and class labels on the image to visualize the detected objects.

Example: Object Detection with YOLO and OpenCV

Python

```python
import cv2

import numpy as np


# Load the YOLO model
net = cv2.dnn.readNet("yolov3.weights", "yolov3.cfg")


# Load the class labels
with open("coco.names", "r") as f:
    classes = [line.strip() for line in f.readlines()]


# Load an image or capture a frame from the camera
image = cv2.imread("image.jpg")
height, width, _ = image.shape
```

Pre-process the image

```
blob = cv2.dnn.blobFromImage(image, 1/255, (416, 416), (0, 0,
0), swapRB=True, crop=False)

net.setInput(blob)
```

Get the detection results

```
output_layers_names = net.getUnconnectedOutLayersNames()

layerOutputs = net.forward(output_layers_names)
```

Post-processing

```
boxes = []

confidences = []

class_ids = []


for output in layerOutputs:

    for detection in output:

        scores = detection[5:]

        class_id = np.argmax(scores)

        confidence = scores[class_id]
```

```python
        if confidence > 0.5:

            center_x = int(detection[0]  width)

            center_y = int(detection[1]  height)

            w = int(detection[2]  width)

            h = int(detection[3]  height)

            x = int(center_x - w / 2)

            y = int(center_y - h / 2)

            boxes.append([x, y, w, h])

            confidences.append(float(confidence))

            class_ids.append(class_id)


 Apply non-maximum suppression
indexes = cv2.dnn.NMSBoxes(boxes, confidences, 0.5, 0.4)


 Draw the bounding boxes and class labels
font = cv2.FONT_HERSHEY_PLAIN
colors = np.random.uniform(0, 255, size=(len(classes), 3))


for i in indexes.flatten():
    x, y, w, h = boxes[i]
```

```
label = str(classes[class_ids[i]])

confidence = str(round(confidences[i], 2))

color = colors[class_ids[i]]

cv2.rectangle(image, (x, y), (x + w, y + h), color, 2)

 cv2.putText(image, label + " " + confidence, (x, y + 20), font,
2, color, 2)



 Display the resulting image

cv2.imshow("Object Detection", image)

cv2.waitKey(0)

cv2.destroyAllWindows()
```

This example demonstrates how to use YOLO and OpenCV to detect objects in an image. It loads the YOLO model, pre-processes the image, performs inference, applies non-maximum suppression, and then visualizes the detected objects by drawing bounding boxes and class labels.

Pose Estimation with MediaPipe

Pose estimation is like giving your AR application the ability to "see" and understand human poses. It involves identifying and tracking key body joints (like shoulders, elbows, wrists) in images or video streams, enabling your AR creations to interact with human movements and gestures.

MediaPipe

MediaPipe is a powerful open-source framework developed by Google for building cross-platform machine learning solutions. It provides a collection of ready-to-use solutions for various tasks, including pose estimation.

- MediaPipe Pose: The MediaPipe Pose solution provides a fast and accurate pose estimation model that can track 33 keypoints on the human body in real-time.

Integrating MediaPipe with OpenCV

You can integrate MediaPipe with OpenCV to perform pose estimation in your AR applications. Here's a simplified workflow:

1. Initialize the MediaPipe Pose Solution: Initialize the MediaPipe Pose solution with the desired parameters (e.g., model complexity, detection confidence).

2. Capture a Frame: Capture a frame from the camera or load an image.
3. Pre-process the Image: Convert the image to RGB format and flip it horizontally if needed.
4. Inference: Pass the pre-processed image through the MediaPipe Pose model to obtain the pose landmarks (keypoint coordinates and visibility scores).
5. Visualization: Draw the pose landmarks and connections on the image to visualize the detected pose.

Example: Pose Estimation with MediaPipe and OpenCV

Python

```
import cv2

import mediapipe as mp


 Initialize the MediaPipe Pose solution

mp_pose = mp.solutions.pose

pose        =        mp_pose.Pose(static_image_mode=False,
min_detection_confidence=0.5, min_tracking_confidence=0.5)
```

```
Open the default camera
cap = cv2.VideoCapture(0)

while True:
    Capture frame-by-frame
    ret, frame = cap.read()

    Pre-process the image
    image = cv2.cvtColor(frame, cv2.COLOR_BGR2RGB)
    image.flags.writeable = False
    results = pose.process(image)
    image.flags.writeable = True
    image = cv2.cvtColor(image, cv2.COLOR_RGB2BGR)

    Draw the pose landmarks
    mp_drawing = mp.solutions.drawing_utils
    mp_drawing_styles = mp.solutions.drawing_styles
    if results.pose_landmarks:
        mp_drawing.draw_landmarks(
            image,
```

```
        results.pose_landmarks,

        mp_pose.POSE_CONNECTIONS,


landmark_drawing_spec=mp_drawing_styles.get_default_pose_l
andmarks_style())


    Display the resulting frame

    cv2.imshow("Pose Estimation", image)


    Break the loop when 'q' is pressed

    if cv2.waitKey(1) & 0xFF == ord('q'):

        break


 When everything done, release the capture

cap.release()

cv2.destroyAllWindows()
```

This example demonstrates how to use MediaPipe and OpenCV to perform pose estimation in a live video stream. It initializes the MediaPipe Pose solution, captures frames from the camera, pre-processes the images, performs inference, and then visualizes the detected pose by drawing landmarks and connections.

Building AI-Powered AR Experiences

By integrating machine learning with AR, you can create truly intelligent and interactive experiences that respond to the environment and user actions in dynamic ways.

Object-Aware AR

Imagine AR applications that can recognize and interact with specific objects in the real world. This could enable experiences like:

- Interactive Product Demonstrations: An AR app that recognizes a product and overlays interactive instructions or animations.
- Object-Specific Information: An AR app that recognizes a landmark and provides historical information or points of interest.
- Context-Aware AR Games: AR games that adapt to the objects and environment around the user.

Pose-Driven AR

Imagine AR applications that can track human poses and gestures to control virtual objects or trigger actions. This could enable experiences like:

- Virtual Try-on with Pose Tracking: An AR app that allows users to try on clothes virtually and see how they fit as they move.
- Gesture-Controlled AR Games: AR games that allow users to control characters or objects with hand gestures.
- Interactive AR Training: AR training applications that track user movements and provide feedback on their form or technique.

Combining ML Techniques

You can combine multiple machine learning techniques to create even more sophisticated AR experiences. For example, you could use object detection to identify a person, pose estimation to track their movements, and then use this information to place virtual objects or effects around them.

Example: AI-Powered AR Game

Python

This is a conceptual example

```
import cv2

... (Object detection with YOLO and pose estimation with
MediaPipe code) ...

while True:

    ... (Capture frame, detect objects and poses) ...


    if person_detected:

        Get the person's pose landmarks

        pose_landmarks = get_pose_landmarks(frame)

        if pose_landmarks:

            Check if the person is raising their hand

            if is_hand_raised(pose_landmarks):

                    Trigger an action in the AR scene (e.g., launch a
virtual projectile)

                    launch_projectile()


    ... (Display the AR scene) ...
```

This example demonstrates how you might combine
object detection and pose estimation to create an
AI-powered AR game. It detects a person, tracks their

pose, and then triggers an action in the AR scene when the person raises their hand.

Code Challenge: AR Object Labeling

Let's create an AR application that can recognize objects and label them in real-time!

Objective: Create an AR application that uses YOLO to detect objects in the camera feed and then overlays labels on those objects, providing information about what they are.

Tools: OpenCV, YOLO model, camera.

Steps:

1. Object Detection: Use YOLO to detect objects in the camera feed.
2. Labeling: Overlay labels on the detected objects, displaying their class names (e.g., "person," "car," "dog").
3. Real-time Updates: Update the labels in real-time as the camera moves or new objects enter the scene.

This challenge will allow you to create an informative AR experience that leverages object detection to provide real-time information about the environment.

Congratulations! You've now explored the exciting world of integrating machine learning with AR. You can use YOLO and TensorFlow for object detection and recognition, MediaPipe for pose estimation, and combine these techniques to build AI-powered AR experiences. Keep experimenting and pushing the boundaries of what's possible with AR!

Chapter 10: The Magic of Faces: Facial Recognition and AR Effects

Prepare to unlock the secrets of the human face and create captivating AR experiences that respond to facial expressions and features! In this chapter, we'll delve into the fascinating world of facial recognition, learn how to detect facial landmarks and analyze expressions in real-time, and discover how to apply stunning AR filters and effects.

By the end, you'll be able to create AR applications that can recognize faces, track facial movements, and enhance or augment facial features with interactive and dynamic effects. Let's embark on this journey of facial AR magic!

Facial Landmark Detection

Facial landmark detection is like mapping the constellations of the human face. It involves identifying key points on the face, such as the eyes, nose, mouth, eyebrows, and jawline. These landmarks provide a framework for understanding facial structure and expressions.

Why Facial Landmarks Matter

Facial landmarks are essential for various AR applications, including:

- Face Tracking: Tracking the movement of the face in real-time to apply AR effects that move with the user's head.
- Facial Expression Analysis: Analyzing the position and movement of landmarks to detect emotions or expressions.
- Facial Feature Enhancement: Augmenting or modifying facial features, such as applying virtual makeup or adding accessories.
- Face Recognition: Identifying individuals based on their unique facial features.

Facial Landmark Detection Methods

There are several approaches to facial landmark detection:

- Traditional Computer Vision Techniques: These methods use image processing techniques and algorithms like Viola-Jones for face detection and then apply geometric models or feature-based approaches to locate landmarks.
- Deep Learning-based Methods: Deep learning models, particularly Convolutional Neural

Networks (CNNs), have revolutionized facial landmark detection, achieving impressive accuracy and robustness.

MediaPipe Face Mesh

MediaPipe Face Mesh is a powerful and efficient solution for facial landmark detection. It uses a machine learning model to accurately detect 468 3D landmarks on the face in real-time, even with challenging lighting conditions or head movements.

Integrating MediaPipe Face Mesh with OpenCV

You can integrate MediaPipe Face Mesh with OpenCV to perform facial landmark detection in your AR applications. Here's a simplified workflow:

1. Initialize the MediaPipe Face Mesh Solution: Initialize the MediaPipe Face Mesh solution with the desired parameters (e.g., maximum number of faces, detection confidence).
2. Capture a Frame: Capture a frame from the camera or load an image.
3. Pre-process the Image: Convert the image to RGB format and flip it horizontally if needed.
4. Inference: Pass the pre-processed image through the MediaPipe Face Mesh model to obtain the facial landmarks (3D coordinates of keypoints).

5. Visualization: Draw the facial landmarks on the image to visualize the detected points.

Example: Facial Landmark Detection with MediaPipe and OpenCV

Python

```
import cv2

import mediapipe as mp


Initialize the MediaPipe Face Mesh solution

mp_face_mesh = mp.solutions.face_mesh

face_mesh = mp_face_mesh.FaceMesh(max_num_faces=1,
refine_landmarks=True, min_detection_confidence=0.5,
min_tracking_confidence=0.5)


Open the default camera

cap = cv2.VideoCapture(0)


while True:

    Capture frame-by-frame

    ret, frame = cap.read()
```

```
Pre-process the image

image = cv2.cvtColor(frame, cv2.COLOR_BGR2RGB)

image.flags.writeable = False

results = face_mesh.process(image)

image.flags.writeable = True

image = cv2.cvtColor(image, cv2.COLOR_RGB2BGR)


Draw the facial landmarks

if results.multi_face_landmarks:

    for facial_landmarks in results.multi_face_landmarks:

        mp_drawing = mp.solutions.drawing_utils

        mp_drawing_styles = mp.solutions.drawing_styles

        mp_drawing.draw_landmarks(

            image=image,

            landmark_list=facial_landmarks,

connections=mp_face_mesh.FACEMESH_TESSELATION,

            landmark_drawing_spec=None,
```

```
connection_drawing_spec=mp_drawing_styles.get_default_face
_mesh_tesselation_style())

    mp_drawing.draw_landmarks(

    image=image,

    landmark_list=facial_landmarks,

connections=mp_face_mesh.FACEMESH_CONTOURS,

    landmark_drawing_spec=None,

connection_drawing_spec=mp_drawing_styles.get_default_face
_mesh_contours_style())


   Display the resulting frame
   cv2.imshow("Facial Landmark Detection", image)


   Break the loop when 'q' is pressed
   if cv2.waitKey(1) & 0xFF == ord('q'):
       break


 When everything done, release the capture
cap.release()
```

```
cv2.destroyAllWindows()
```

This example demonstrates how to use MediaPipe Face Mesh and OpenCV to detect facial landmarks in a live video stream. It initializes the MediaPipe Face Mesh solution, captures frames from the camera, pre-processes the images, performs inference, and then visualizes the detected landmarks by drawing them on the image.

Real-time Facial Expression Analysis

Facial expression analysis is like reading the emotions and intentions hidden within the subtle movements of the human face. It involves analyzing facial landmarks and their dynamics to recognize expressions like happiness, sadness, anger, surprise, and more.

Why Facial Expression Analysis Matters

Facial expression analysis has numerous applications in AR, including:

- Emotionally Responsive AR: Creating AR experiences that adapt to the user's emotions, providing personalized content or feedback.

- Interactive Storytelling: Developing AR narratives where characters or environments react to the user's expressions.
- Accessibility Features: Building AR tools that can assist people with communication difficulties by recognizing their expressions.
- Gaming and Entertainment: Creating AR games or experiences that respond to the player's emotions or expressions.

Analyzing Facial Expressions

Facial expression analysis typically involves the following steps:

1. Facial Landmark Detection: Detect facial landmarks using techniques like MediaPipe Face Mesh.
2. Feature Extraction: Extract relevant features from the landmark data, such as distances between landmarks, angles, or movement patterns.
3. Expression Classification: Use a machine learning model (like a Support Vector Machine or a Neural Network) to classify the extracted features into different expressions.

Building an Expression Analyzer

You can build your own facial expression analyzer using OpenCV and a machine learning library like scikit-learn. Here's a simplified workflow:

1. Collect Training Data: Gather a dataset of images or videos with labeled facial expressions.
2. Extract Features: Extract relevant features from the facial landmarks in the training data.
3. Train a Classifier: Train a machine learning classifier (e.g., SVM) on the extracted features and their corresponding labels.
4. Real-time Analysis: In your AR application, detect facial landmarks, extract features, and use the trained classifier to predict the user's expression in real-time.

Example: Simple Expression Analysis with OpenCV and scikit-learn

Python

```
import cv2
from sklearn.svm import SVC


... (Facial landmark detection code) ...


Define a function to extract features from facial landmarks
```

```
def extract_features(landmarks):

    ... (Calculate distances, angles, or other relevant features from
    the landmarks) ...

    return features


Load the trained SVM classifier

classifier = SVC()

classifier = joblib.load("expression_classifier.pkl")


while True:

    ... (Capture frame and detect facial landmarks) ...


    if facial_landmarks:

        Extract features from the landmarks

        features = extract_features(facial_landmarks)


        Predict the expression using the trained classifier

        expression = classifier.predict([features])[0]


        Display the predicted expression on the image
```

```
        cv2.putText(image, expression, (100, 100),
cv2.FONT_HERSHEY_SIMPLEX, 1, (0, 255, 0), 2)
```

... (Display the AR scene) ...

This example demonstrates how to use OpenCV and
scikit-learn to build a simple facial expression analyzer.
It extracts features from the detected facial landmarks
and then uses a trained SVM classifier to predict the
user's expression in real-time.

Applying AR Filters and Effects

AR filters and effects are like digital makeup or masks
that can enhance or augment facial features in real-time.
They can add virtual accessories, change hair color,
apply makeup, or even transform the user's face into a
different character.

Types of AR Filters and Effects

AR filters and effects can range from simple overlays to
complex transformations:

- Virtual Makeup: Apply virtual lipstick,
  eyeshadow, or other makeup to the user's face.

177

- Accessories: Add virtual glasses, hats, or jewelry to the user's face.
- Facial Feature Modification: Change the shape or size of facial features, such as enlarging eyes or slimming the face.
- Face Swapping: Swap the user's face with another face (e.g., a celebrity or a character).
- Animated Effects: Add animated elements to the face, such as sparkling eyes or moving eyebrows.

Applying Filters and Effects with OpenCV

OpenCV, combined with facial landmark detection, provides the tools to apply AR filters and effects. Here's a simplified workflow:

1. Detect Facial Landmarks: Detect facial landmarks using techniques like MediaPipe Face Mesh.
2. Align the Filter: Align the AR filter or effect with the detected facial landmarks, ensuring it moves and rotates with the user's head.
3. Blending and Rendering: Blend the filter or effect with the user's face, creating a seamless and realistic appearance.

Example: Applying a Virtual Hat

Python

```python
import cv2

... (Facial landmark detection code) ...

Load the hat image
hat_image                    =                cv2.imread("hat.png",
cv2.IMREAD_UNCHANGED)


while True:
    ... (Capture frame and detect facial landmarks) ...


    if facial_landmarks:
        Get the coordinates of the top of the head
            top_head_x = int(facial_landmarks.landmark[10].x
image.shape[1])

            top_head_y = int(facial_landmarks.landmark[10].y
image.shape[0])


        Resize the hat image
        hat_width = int(hat_image.shape[1] 0.2)

        hat_height = int(hat_image.shape[0] 0.2)
```

```
        resized_hat = cv2.resize(hat_image, (hat_width,
hat_height))


    Overlay the hat on the image

    overlay_image(image, resized_hat, top_head_x - hat_width
// 2, top_head_y - hat_height)


    ... (Display the AR scene) ...
```

This example demonstrates how to apply a virtual hat to the user's head using OpenCV and facial landmark detection. It detects the top of the head using the facial landmarks and then overlays a resized hat image on that position.

Code Challenge: AR Face Mask

Let's create an AR application that applies a fun and interactive face mask!

Objective: Create an AR application that detects the user's face and applies a virtual mask that moves and rotates with their head. Allow the user to switch between different masks or add animated effects.

Tools: OpenCV, MediaPipe Face Mesh, mask images or 3D models, camera.

Steps:

1. Facial Landmark Detection: Detect facial landmarks using MediaPipe Face Mesh.
2. Mask Alignment: Align the virtual mask with the detected facial landmarks.
3. Mask Switching: Allow the user to switch between different masks using keyboard input or touch gestures.
4. Animated Effects: Add animated effects to the mask, such as glowing eyes or moving parts.

This challenge will allow you to create a playful and engaging AR experience that combines facial landmark detection, image manipulation, and user interaction.

Congratulations! You've now explored the fascinating world of facial recognition and AR effects. You can detect facial landmarks, analyze expressions, and apply AR filters and effects to create interactive and engaging AR experiences. Keep experimenting and pushing the boundaries of what's possible with facial AR!

Chapter 11: Beyond the Image: 3D Reconstruction and Environment Understanding

Prepare to step into the third dimension and unlock a deeper understanding of the world around you! In this chapter, we'll explore the fascinating techniques of 3D reconstruction, which allow your AR applications to not just see, but to truly perceive the environment in three dimensions. We'll delve into depth estimation with stereo vision, explore the magic of Structure from Motion (SfM), and learn how to process and visualize 3D point clouds with Open3D.

By the end, you'll be able to create AR experiences that go beyond simple overlays, enabling virtual objects to interact with the real world in more realistic and immersive ways. Let's embark on this journey of 3D perception and environment understanding!

Depth Estimation with Stereo Vision

Stereo vision is like giving your AR application a pair of eyes, allowing it to perceive depth and distance just as humans do. It involves using two cameras to capture slightly different views of the same scene and then analyzing the differences between those views to estimate the depth of objects in the scene.

How Stereo Vision Works

The basic principle behind stereo vision is triangulation. By comparing the positions of corresponding points in the two camera images, we can calculate the distance to those points in the 3D world.

Here's a simplified overview of the process:

1. Camera Calibration: Calibrate the two cameras to determine their intrinsic parameters (focal length, principal point) and extrinsic parameters (relative position and orientation).
2. Image Rectification: Transform the two images so that corresponding epipolar lines (lines connecting corresponding points) become parallel. This simplifies the search for corresponding points.
3. Correspondence Matching: Find matching points in the two rectified images. This is typically done using feature matching techniques or correlation-based methods.
4. Depth Calculation: Calculate the depth of the matched points using triangulation. The disparity

(difference in position) between corresponding points is inversely proportional to the depth.

Depth Maps

The result of stereo vision is a depth map, which is an image where each pixel represents the distance from the camera to the corresponding point in the scene. Depth maps provide valuable information about the 3D structure of the environment.

Applications of Stereo Vision

Stereo vision has numerous applications in AR and robotics, including:

- Obstacle Avoidance. Robots or AR devices can use depth information to avoid collisions with objects in the environment.
- 3D Reconstruction: Depth maps can be used to create 3D models of objects or environments.
- Augmented Reality: Depth information can be used to place virtual objects more realistically in the AR scene and enable interactions with the real world.

OpenCV for Stereo Vision

OpenCV provides several functions and tools for stereo vision, including:

- **Camera Calibration:** cv2.calibrateCamera()
- **Image Rectification:** cv2.stereoRectify()
- **Stereo Matching:** cv2.StereoBM_create(), cv2.StereoSGBM_create()

Example: Depth Estimation with OpenCV

Python

```python
import cv2

import numpy as np


Load the camera calibration parameters
camera_matrix_left = np.load("camera_matrix_left.npy")

dist_coeffs_left = np.load("dist_coeffs_left.npy")

camera_matrix_right = np.load("camera_matrix_right.npy")

dist_coeffs_right = np.load("dist_coeffs_right.npy")


Load the stereo rectification parameters
R1 = np.load("R1.npy")

R2 = np.load("R2.npy")
```

```python
P1 = np.load("P1.npy")

P2 = np.load("P2.npy")

Q = np.load("Q.npy")


Create a stereo matcher object

stereo         =         cv2.StereoSGBM_create(minDisparity=0,
numDisparities=163, blockSize=15)


Open the left and right cameras

cap_left = cv2.VideoCapture(0)

cap_right = cv2.VideoCapture(1)


while True:

    Capture frames from both cameras

    ret_left, frame_left = cap_left.read()

    ret_right, frame_right = cap_right.read()


    Rectify the images

    imgL = cv2.remap(frame_left, R1, P1, cv2.INTER_LINEAR)
```

```python
        imgR = cv2.remap(frame_right, R2, P2,
cv2.INTER_LINEAR)


    Convert to grayscale
    grayL = cv2.cvtColor(imgL, cv2.COLOR_BGR2GRAY)
    grayR = cv2.cvtColor(imgR, cv2.COLOR_BGR2GRAY)


    Compute the disparity map
    disparity = stereo.compute(grayL, grayR)


    Normalize the disparity map for visualization
    disparity = cv2.normalize(disparity, None, alpha=0, beta=255,
norm_type=cv2.NORM_MINMAX, dtype=cv2.CV_8U)


    Display the disparity map
    cv2.imshow("Disparity Map", disparity)


    Break the loop when 'q' is pressed
    if cv2.waitKey(1) & 0xFF == ord('q'):
        break
```

When everything done, release the captures

cap_left.release()

cap_right.release()

cv2.destroyAllWindows()

This example demonstrates how to use OpenCV to estimate depth from a pair of stereo cameras. It loads the camera calibration and rectification parameters, creates a stereo matcher object, captures frames from both cameras, rectifies the images, computes the disparity map, and then displays it for visualization.

Structure from Motion (SfM)

Structure from Motion (SfM) is like reconstructing a 3D puzzle from a collection of 2D photographs. It involves analyzing a sequence of images taken from different viewpoints and then extracting 3D structure and camera poses from those images.

How SfM Works

SfM algorithms typically follow these steps:

1. Feature Detection and Matching: Detect and match features (like corners or edges) across multiple images.
2. Structure Estimation: Estimate the 3D positions of the matched features using triangulation or bundle adjustment techniques.
3. Camera Pose Estimation: Estimate the camera pose (position and orientation) for each image.
4. Scene Optimization: Refine the 3D structure and camera poses to minimize errors and create a consistent 3D model.

Applications of SfM

SfM has various applications in AR, computer vision, and 3D modeling:

- 3D Reconstruction: Creating 3D models of objects or environments from photographs.
- Virtual Tours: Generating immersive virtual tours of real-world locations.
- Augmented Reality: Using SfM to create 3D maps of the environment for more realistic and interactive AR experiences.

SfM Libraries and Tools

Several libraries and tools are available for performing SfM, including:

- OpenMVG (Open Multiple View Geometry): An open-source library for SfM.
- OpenMVS (Open Multiple View Stereo): An open-source library for dense 3D reconstruction from SfM outputs.
- VisualSFM: A GUI-based tool for SfM.
- Colmap: A general-purpose Structure-from-Motion and Multi-View Stereo pipeline with a graphical and command-line interface.

Example: SfM with OpenMVG and OpenMVS

Bash

This is a conceptual example using command-line tools

Run OpenMVG to extract features and estimate camera poses

openMVG_main_SfMInit_ImageListing -i image_folder -o output_folder -d sensor_width_database.txt

openMVG_main_ComputeFeatures -i output_folder/sfm_data.json -o output_folder -m SIFT -p HIGH

openMVG_main_ComputeMatches -i output_folder/sfm_data.json -o output_folder -g e

```
openMVG_main_IncrementalSfM                              -i
output_folder/sfm_data.json -m output_folder -o output_folder
```

Run OpenMVS to perform dense reconstruction

```
openMVS_main_InterfaceCOLMAP                              -i
output_folder/sfm_data.bin -o output_folder/scene.mvs
```

```
openMVS_main_DensifyPointCloud -i output_folder/scene.mvs
-o output_folder/scene_dense.mvs
```

```
openMVS_main_ReconstructMesh                             -i
output_folder/scene_dense.mvs                            -o
output_folder/scene_mesh.mvs
```

This example demonstrates how to use OpenMVG and OpenMVS to perform SfM and dense 3D reconstruction from a set of images. It uses command-line tools to extract features, estimate camera poses, and then generate a dense point cloud and a mesh.

Point Cloud Processing with Open3D

Point clouds are collections of 3D points that represent the surface of an object or environment. They are a common output of 3D reconstruction techniques like stereo vision and SfM. Open3D is a powerful open-source library for processing and visualizing point clouds.

Open3D Features

Open3D provides a wide range of functionalities for point cloud processing, including:

- Visualization: Visualize point clouds in 3D with various rendering options.
- Filtering: Remove noise and outliers from point clouds.
- Segmentation: Divide point clouds into meaningful segments or clusters.
- Registration: Align multiple point clouds to create a complete 3D model.
- Surface Reconstruction: Create mesh models from point clouds.

Example: Visualizing a Point Cloud with Open3D

Python

```
import open3d as o3d
```

Load the point cloud

```
pcd = o3d.io.read_point_cloud("point_cloud.ply")
```

Visualize the point cloud

```
o3d.visualization.draw_geometries([pcd])
```

This example demonstrates how to load and visualize a point cloud using Open3D. It reads a point cloud from a PLY file and then displays it in a 3D viewer.

Example: Point Cloud Filtering and Segmentation

Python

```
import open3d as o3d
```

Load the point cloud

```
pcd = o3d.io.read_point_cloud("noisy_point_cloud.ply")
```

Downsample the point cloud

```
downpcd = pcd.voxel_down_sample(voxel_size=0.05)
```

Remove statistical outliers

```python
cl, ind = downpcd.remove_statistical_outlier(nb_neighbors=20,
std_ratio=2.0)

inlier_cloud = downpcd.select_by_index(ind)
```

Segment the point cloud using DBSCAN clustering

```python
with
o3d.utility.VerbosityContextManager(o3d.utility.VerbosityLevel.
Debug) as cm:
        labels = np.array(inlier_cloud.cluster_dbscan(eps=0.5,
min_points=10, print_progress=True))
```

Color the point cloud based on the labels

```python
max_label = labels.max()

colors = plt.get_cmap("tab20")(labels / (max_label if max_label
> 0 else 1))

colors[labels < 0] = 0

inlier_cloud.colors = o3d.utility.Vector3dVector(colors[:, :3])
```

Visualize the segmented point cloud

```python
o3d.visualization.draw_geometries([inlier_cloud])
```

This example demonstrates how to filter and segment a point cloud using Open3D. It downsamples the point cloud, removes statistical outliers, and then segments it using DBSCAN clustering. The segmented point cloud is visualized with different colors for each cluster.

Code Challenge: 3D Environment Reconstruction

Let's combine your knowledge of 3D reconstruction techniques to create a 3D model of your environment!

Objective: Capture a sequence of images of your environment using a camera and then use SfM to reconstruct a 3D model of the scene. Visualize the reconstructed point cloud or mesh using Open3D.

Tools: OpenCV, OpenMVG, OpenMVS (or other SfM libraries), Open3D, camera.

Steps:

1. Image Capture: Capture a sequence of images of your environment from different viewpoints, ensuring sufficient overlap between images.

2. SfM Reconstruction: Use OpenMVG (or another SfM library) to process the images and generate a sparse 3D point cloud and camera poses.
3. Dense Reconstruction: (Optional) Use OpenMVS (or another dense reconstruction library) to generate a dense point cloud from the sparse reconstruction.
4. Point Cloud Processing: (Optional) Use Open3D to process the point cloud, removing noise, outliers, or performing segmentation.
5. Visualization: Visualize the reconstructed point cloud or mesh using Open3D.

This challenge will allow you to apply your knowledge of stereo vision, SfM, and point cloud processing to create a 3D model of your surroundings.

Congratulations! You've now delved into the world of 3D reconstruction and environment understanding. You can estimate depth with stereo vision, reconstruct 3D scenes with SfM, and process point clouds with Open3D. You're well-equipped to create AR experiences that go beyond simple overlays, enabling virtual objects to interact with the real world in more realistic and immersive ways. Keep exploring and pushing the boundaries of AR!

Part VI: Building Real-World AR Applications

Chapter 12: Level Up Your Skills: Developing an AR Game

Get ready to bring your AR knowledge to life and create your very own interactive game! In this chapter, we'll combine the skills you've learned so far to develop an engaging AR game. We'll cover the essentials of game design and mechanics, delve into object interaction and collision detection, design user interfaces and controls, and explore techniques for optimizing performance.

By the end, you'll have the tools and knowledge to build your own AR games that blend the real and virtual worlds, creating immersive and entertaining experiences. Let's embark on this game development adventure!

Game Design and Mechanics

Before diving into code, every great AR game starts with a solid foundation in game design and mechanics. This is where you define the core gameplay loop, the rules of the game, and the overall player experience.

Core Gameplay Loop

The core gameplay loop is the heart of your game. It's the cycle of actions that players repeat throughout the game, keeping them engaged and entertained. A well-designed gameplay loop should be:

- Challenging: Provides a sense of accomplishment when players overcome obstacles.
- Rewarding: Offers incentives and feedback for player progress.
- Engaging: Keeps players interested and motivated to continue playing.

Examples of core gameplay loops in AR games:

- Explore and Collect: Players explore the real world to find and collect virtual objects (e.g., Pokémon Go).
- Build and Defend: Players build structures and defend them from virtual enemies (e.g., Minecraft Earth).
- Puzzle Solving: Players solve puzzles by interacting with virtual objects in the real world.

Game Mechanics

Game mechanics are the rules and systems that govern how the game works. They define how players interact with the game world, how objects behave, and how challenges are presented.

Examples of game mechanics in AR games:

- Movement and Navigation: How players move through the AR environment (e.g., walking, teleporting).
- Object Interaction: How players interact with virtual objects (e.g., tapping, dragging, throwing).
- Combat: How players engage in combat with virtual enemies (e.g., shooting, casting spells).
- Resource Management: How players manage resources like health, energy, or currency.

Designing for AR

When designing an AR game, consider the unique aspects of the AR medium:

- Real-World Integration: Integrate the game with the player's real-world environment, using location-based features or environmental interactions.
- Player Movement: Encourage player movement and exploration in the real world.
- Social Interaction: (Optional) Incorporate social features that allow players to interact with each other in the AR space.

Prototyping and Iteration

Game design is an iterative process. Start with a simple prototype to test your core gameplay loop and mechanics. Then, gather feedback and iterate on your design to improve the player experience.

Example: Designing an AR Target Shooting Game

Imagine an AR target shooting game where players use their phone's camera to aim and shoot virtual targets that appear in the real world.

- Core Gameplay Loop:
    - Targets appear in the environment.
    - Player aims and shoots at the targets.
    - Player scores points for hitting targets.
    - Difficulty increases over time.
- Game Mechanics:
    - Target Spawning: Targets spawn at random locations in the environment.
    - Aiming and Shooting: Players use their phone's camera to aim and tap the screen to shoot.
    - Projectile Trajectory: Simulate projectile motion with gravity and air resistance.
    - Scoring: Award points based on accuracy and speed.

Object Interaction and Collision Detection

Object interaction and collision detection are essential for creating engaging and believable AR games. They allow players to interact with virtual objects in the real world and ensure that those objects behave realistically.

Interaction Methods

There are various ways for players to interact with virtual objects in AR games:

- Touch Input: Tapping, dragging, or swiping on the screen to interact with objects.
- Motion Controls: Using the device's accelerometer or gyroscope to control object movement or orientation.
- Voice Commands: Using voice commands to interact with objects or trigger actions.

Collision Detection

Collision detection algorithms determine whether two or more objects are intersecting in the 3D space of your AR game. This is crucial for:

- Preventing Clipping: Ensuring that virtual objects don't pass through each other or real-world surfaces.

- Triggering Actions: Detecting when objects collide to trigger events or actions (e.g., a ball bouncing off a wall, a player picking up an item).

Collision Detection Techniques

- Bounding Boxes: A simple and efficient approach is to use bounding boxes (rectangular boxes that enclose objects) to detect collisions.
- More Advanced Techniques: For more complex shapes, you can use techniques like ray casting or mesh-based collision detection.

Physics Engines

Physics engines, like Bullet or PhysX, can be integrated with your AR game to simulate realistic physics interactions. This allows you to:

- Simulate Gravity: Make objects fall realistically.
- Handle Collisions: Resolve collisions between objects, applying forces and impulses.
- Simulate Friction: Affect how objects slide or roll on surfaces.

Example: Interactive Ball Game

Imagine an AR game where players can throw a virtual ball and watch it bounce off real-world surfaces.

- Interaction: Players use touch input to "throw" the ball with different forces and directions.
- Collision Detection: Use collision detection to detect when the ball hits a real-world surface (detected using plane detection) or another virtual object.
- Physics Simulation: Use a physics engine to simulate the ball's trajectory, gravity, and collisions with surfaces.

User Interface and Controls

A well-designed user interface (UI) and intuitive controls are crucial for a positive player experience. They should be clear, easy to use, and not obstruct the AR view.

UI Elements

Common UI elements in AR games include:

- Score Display: Shows the player's score or progress.
- Health/Energy Bars: Displays the player's health or energy levels.
- Menus and Buttons: Provides access to settings, options, or in-game actions.

- Instructions and Feedback: Provides clear instructions and feedback to the player.

Control Schemes

Choose control schemes that are appropriate for the AR platform and the type of game.

- Touch Input: For mobile AR games, touch input is the primary control method. Use gestures like tapping, swiping, and dragging to control actions.
- Motion Controls: Utilize the device's accelerometer or gyroscope for motion-based controls.
- Voice Commands: (Optional) Incorporate voice commands for hands-free control.

UI Design Considerations

- Minimalism: Keep the UI clean and minimal to avoid cluttering the AR view.
- Clarity: Use clear and concise visuals and text.
- Responsiveness: Ensure that the UI is responsive and provides immediate feedback to the player's actions.
- Accessibility: Consider accessibility for players with disabilities.

Example: AR Target Shooting UI

In the AR target shooting game example, the UI could include:

- Crosshair: A crosshair in the center of the screen to aid aiming.
- Score Display: A display showing the player's current score.
- Ammo Counter: (Optional) A counter showing the remaining ammunition.
- Reload Button: (Optional) A button to reload the weapon.

Optimizing for Performance

AR games often require significant processing power to render graphics, track objects, and perform AI tasks in real-time. Optimizing performance is crucial for ensuring smooth gameplay and a positive player experience.

Performance Bottlenecks

Common performance bottlenecks in AR games include:

- Rendering: Rendering 3D graphics can be computationally expensive.
- Computer Vision: Object detection, tracking, and other computer vision tasks can consume significant processing power.

- Physics Simulation: Simulating physics interactions can also be computationally demanding.

Optimization Techniques

- Efficient Rendering: Use optimized 3D models, reduce polygon count, and utilize techniques like level of detail (LOD) rendering to render objects with varying levels of detail based on their distance from the camera.
- Computer Vision Optimization: Use efficient computer vision algorithms, optimize image resolution, and consider using hardware acceleration for computer vision tasks.
- Physics Engine Optimization: Use appropriate physics engine settings, simplify collision shapes, and reduce the number of physics objects in the scene.
- Code Optimization: Write efficient code, avoid unnecessary calculations, and use profiling tools to identify performance bottlenecks in your code.

Performance Testing and Profiling

Regularly test your game's performance on different devices and use profiling tools to identify areas that need optimization.

Example: Optimizing the AR Ball Game

In the AR ball game example, you could optimize performance by:

- Simplifying the Ball's Collision Shape: Use a simple sphere collider instead of a complex mesh collider for the ball.
- Reducing the Number of Physics Objects: Limit the number of balls or other physics objects in the scene.
- Optimizing the Rendering of the Environment: Use simple geometry for the environment or apply texture compression to reduce rendering overhead.

Code Challenge: AR Basketball Game

Let's combine all the elements of this chapter to create an AR basketball game!

Objective: Develop an AR game where players can shoot virtual basketballs into a real-world hoop.

Tools: OpenCV, a physics engine (like Bullet or PhysX), a camera, a real-world basketball hoop.

Steps:

1. Game Design: Design the core gameplay loop, scoring system, and game mechanics.
2. Object Interaction: Allow players to "pick up" and "throw" the basketball using touch input and motion controls.
3. Collision Detection: Detect collisions between the basketball, the hoop, and the backboard.
4. Physics Simulation: Use a physics engine to simulate the basketball's trajectory and collisions.
5. UI and Controls: Design a user interface that displays the score and provides controls for shooting and resetting the ball.
6. Performance Optimization: Optimize the game's performance for smooth gameplay.

This challenge will allow you to apply your knowledge of game design, object interaction, physics simulation, UI design, and performance optimization to create a fun and engaging AR game.

Congratulations! You've now learned the essential elements of developing an AR game. You can design game mechanics, implement object interaction and collision detection, create user interfaces and controls, and optimize performance. Go forth and create amazing AR games that blend the real and virtual worlds!

Chapter 13: Igniting Curiosity: Creating an Educational AR Experience

Get ready to transform the way we learn and explore with the power of Augmented Reality! In this chapter, we'll delve into the exciting world of educational AR, where complex concepts come to life, interactive learning becomes the norm, and engaging content sparks curiosity and deepens understanding.

By the end, you'll have the knowledge and tools to create AR experiences that revolutionize education, making learning more immersive, interactive, and fun for students of all ages. Let's embark on this journey of educational AR innovation!

Visualizing Complex Concepts in 3D

One of the most powerful applications of AR in education is the ability to visualize complex concepts in 3D. By bringing abstract ideas into the real world as interactive 3D models, AR can make learning more intuitive, engaging, and memorable.

Breaking Down Barriers to Understanding

Traditional teaching methods often rely on 2D representations, like diagrams or illustrations, to explain complex concepts. However, these representations can be challenging for some students to grasp, especially when dealing with 3D structures or dynamic processes.

AR overcomes this limitation by allowing students to interact with virtual 3D models in their own environment. They can rotate, zoom, and dissect these models, exploring them from different angles and gaining a deeper understanding of their structure and function.

Examples of 3D Visualization in AR

- Anatomy: Students can explore the human body in 3D, interacting with organs, muscles, and skeletal structures. They can dissect virtual organs, zoom in to see intricate details, and learn about the interconnectedness of different body systems.
- Chemistry: Students can visualize molecules and chemical reactions in 3D, gaining a better understanding of molecular structures, bonding, and chemical processes. They can manipulate virtual molecules, observe reactions in real-time, and even conduct virtual experiments.

- Physics: Students can explore physics concepts like gravity, motion, and forces through interactive 3D simulations. They can experiment with virtual objects, observe the effects of diffcrent forces, and gain a deeper understanding of physical laws.
- Astronomy: Students can explore the solar system and beyond with 3D models of planets, stars, and galaxies. They can observe planetary orbits, zoom in to see surface details, and learn about celestial phenomena.

Benefits of 3D Visualization

- Improved Understanding: 3D visualization helps students grasp complex concepts more easily by providing a tangible and interactive representation.
- Increased Engagement: Interactive 3D models make learning more engaging and fun, capturing students' attention and motivating them to explore.
- Enhanced Memory Retention: Studies have shown that 3D visualization can improve memory retention by creating a more vivid and memorable learning experience.
- Personalized Learning: AR allows for personalized learning experiences, as students

can explore 3D models at their own pace and focus on areas that interest them.

Creating 3D Models for AR

You can create 3D models for your educational AR experiences using various tools and techniques:

- 3D Modeling Software: Use software like Blender, Maya, or 3ds Max to create your own 3D models.
- Online Model Libraries: Download free or paid 3D models from online libraries like Sketchfab, TurboSquid, or Google Poly.
- Photogrammetry: Create 3D models from photographs using photogrammetry software.

Example: AR Heart Exploration

Imagine an AR application that allows students to explore a 3D model of a human heart.

- Interaction: Students can use touch input to rotate, zoom, and dissect the virtual heart.
- Labels and Information: Labels and information pop up as students interact with different parts of the heart, providing details about their structure and function.

- Animations: Animations show the heart beating and blood flowing through its chambers, providing a dynamic visualization of the circulatory system.

Interactive Learning and Exploration

AR transforms passive learning into active exploration, empowering students to engage with educational content in dynamic and interactive ways. By providing hands-on experiences and personalized learning paths, AR can foster deeper understanding and a love for learning.

Hands-on Experiences

AR allows students to learn by doing, providing hands-on experiences that were previously impossible or impractical. This can involve:

- Virtual Experiments: Conduct virtual experiments in a safe and controlled environment.
- Simulations: Simulate real-world scenarios or processes, such as dissecting a virtual frog or building a virtual circuit.
- Interactive Games: Engage in educational games that challenge students to apply their knowledge and solve problems.

- Virtual Field Trips: Take virtual field trips to museums, historical sites, or even outer space.

Personalized Learning

AR can personalize the learning experience by adapting to individual student needs and preferences. This can involve:

- Adaptive Learning: Adjust the difficulty or pace of the learning content based on student performance.
- Personalized Feedback: Provide individualized feedback and guidance to students.
- Choice and Agency: Allow students to choose their own learning paths and explore topics that interest them.

Collaborative Learning

AR can also foster collaborative learning by providing shared experiences and opportunities for interaction. This can involve:

- Group Projects: Work together on AR projects, such as building a virtual city or designing a virtual ecosystem.
- Shared Experiences: Engage in shared AR experiences, such as exploring a virtual museum

together or collaborating on a virtual science experiment.

- Peer-to-Peer Learning: Learn from each other by sharing knowledge and experiences in an AR environment.

Benefits of Interactive Learning

- Increased Engagement: Interactive learning keeps students engaged and motivated by providing active and stimulating experiences.
- Deeper Understanding: Hands-on experiences and personalized learning paths lead to a deeper understanding of concepts.
- Improved Problem-Solving Skills: Interactive simulations and games challenge students to apply their knowledge and develop problem-solving skills.
- Increased Collaboration: Shared AR experiences foster collaboration and communication skills.

Example: AR Solar System Exploration

Imagine an AR application that allows students to explore the solar system.

- Interaction: Students can use touch input to move around the solar system, zoom in on planets, and even land on their surfaces.

- Information and Facts: Information about each planet pops up as students interact with it, providing details about its size, composition, and atmosphere.
- Quizzes and Challenges: Quizzes and challenges test students' knowledge of the solar system and encourage them to learn more.

Designing Engaging Educational Content

Creating engaging educational content is crucial for capturing students' attention and fostering a love for learning. AR provides a unique opportunity to design interactive and immersive experiences that go beyond traditional textbooks and lectures.

Storytelling and Narrative

Incorporate storytelling and narrative elements to make learning more engaging and memorable. This can involve:

- AR Storybooks: Create interactive storybooks where characters come to life and environments transform around the reader.
- Historical Recreations: Recreate historical events or scenes in AR, allowing students to experience them firsthand.

- Virtual Characters: Introduce virtual characters that guide students through the learning experience, providing explanations and encouragement.

Gamification

Gamification techniques can make learning more fun and motivating. This can involve:

- Points and Rewards: Award points or virtual rewards for completing tasks or achieving goals.
- Challenges and Competitions: Introduce challenges or competitions to encourage students to strive for excellence.
- Leaderboards: Display leaderboards to foster a sense of competition and achievement.

Multisensory Experiences

Engage multiple senses to create a more immersive and memorable learning experience. This can involve:

- Sound Effects: Add sound effects to enhance the AR experience and provide feedback.
- Music: Use music to create atmosphere and evoke emotions.

- Haptic Feedback: (Optional) Incorporate haptic feedback to provide a sense of touch and interaction.

Accessibility and Inclusivity

Design educational AR experiences that are accessible to students with diverse learning styles and needs. This can involve:

- Multiple Modes of Interaction: Provide different modes of interaction, such as touch, voice, or gesture control.
- Customization Options: Allow students to customize the AR experience to their preferences, such as adjusting font sizes or colors.
- Multilingual Support: Offer content in multiple languages to cater to diverse learners.

Example: AR History Lesson

Imagine an AR application that teaches students about ancient Egypt.

- Virtual Tour: Take students on a virtual tour of ancient Egyptian pyramids and temples.
- Interactive Exhibits: Allow students to interact with virtual exhibits, such as examining

hieroglyphics or exploring a 3D model of a pharaoh's tomb.

- Quizzes and Games: Engage students with quizzes and games that test their knowledge of ancient Egyptian history and culture.

Code Challenge: AR Periodic Table

Let's create an interactive AR periodic table that brings chemistry to life!

Objective: Develop an AR application that displays a 3D periodic table where students can interact with elements to learn about their properties and see visual representations of their atomic structures.

Tools: OpenCV, a 3D modeling tool (or online model library), camera.

Steps:

1. 3D Periodic Table: Create a 3D model of the periodic table with interactive elements.
2. Element Information: Display information about each element when it is selected, such as its atomic number, mass, and electron configuration.
3. Atomic Structure Visualization: Show a 3D model of the element's atomic structure when it is selected.

4. Interactive Quizzes: Include interactive quizzes or games that test students' knowledge of the periodic table.

This challenge will allow you to apply your knowledge of 3D visualization, interactive learning, and engaging content design to create an educational AR experience that makes chemistry more accessible and fun.

Congratulations! You've now explored the exciting world of creating educational AR experiences. You can visualize complex concepts in 3D, design interactive learning activities, and create engaging educational content that sparks curiosity and deepens understanding. Go forth and transform the way we learn with the power of AR!

Chapter 14: AR in Your Pocket: Building an AR Utility Application

Prepare to transform your smartphone into a versatile AR toolkit! In this chapter, we'll shift our focus from games and educational experiences to building practical AR utility applications that can enhance your everyday life. We'll explore how to create tools for real-time measurement and navigation, delve into the world of information overlays and data visualization, and discover how AR can be used to solve everyday problems.

By the end, you'll have the knowledge and skills to build AR applications that can help you measure objects, navigate your surroundings, visualize data, and perform various other tasks with the convenience and power of augmented reality. Let's dive into the world of AR utility applications!

Real-time Measurement and Navigation

AR can transform your smartphone into a powerful measurement tool and a personalized navigation guide, enhancing your perception of the world and providing valuable information in real-time.

AR Measurement Tools

Imagine measuring the dimensions of a room, the height of a tree, or the distance between two objects simply by pointing your phone's camera. AR measurement tools make this possible by leveraging computer vision and depth sensing technologies.

- How it Works:
    - Plane Detection: The AR application detects planar surfaces in the environment, such as floors, walls, or objects.
    - Feature Tracking: The application tracks features on the detected planes as the camera moves.
    - Depth Estimation: Using depth sensors or stereo vision techniques, the application estimates the distance to the features.
    - Measurement Calculation: Based on the tracked features and depth information, the application calculates distances, lengths, areas, or volumes.
- Applications:
    - Home Improvement: Measure furniture, appliances, or rooms for renovation projects.
    - Construction: Measure distances and angles on construction sites.

- Design and Planning: Measure objects or spaces for design and planning purposes.
- Education: Use AR measurement tools in classrooms for interactive learning activities.

AR Navigation

AR can enhance traditional navigation systems by overlaying directions and guidance directly onto the real-world view. This can make navigation more intuitive and less distracting, especially in complex or unfamiliar environments.

- How it Works:
  - Location Tracking: The AR application uses GPS or other location tracking technologies to determine the user's position.
  - Sensor Fusion: Data from accelerometers, gyroscopes, and compasses is combined to track the user's orientation and movement.
  - Pathfinding: The application calculates the optimal path to the destination, taking into account obstacles or road conditions.
  - AR Guidance: Directional arrows, virtual paths, or other visual cues are overlaid on the camera view to guide the user.

- Applications:
  - Indoor Navigation: Navigate through complex indoor environments like airports, shopping malls, or museums.
  - Outdoor Navigation: Enhance GPS navigation with AR guidance, providing visual cues and points of interest overlaid on the real-world view.
  - Tourist Guides: Provide tourists with interactive AR tours and information about historical landmarks.

Example: AR Measuring Tape

Imagine an AR application that functions as a virtual measuring tape.

- Interaction: Users tap on the screen to place virtual markers on the starting and ending points of the measurement.
- Measurement Calculation: The application calculates the distance between the markers in real-time, displaying the measurement on the screen.
- Units and Options: Allow users to choose different units (e.g., centimeters, inches, feet) and provide options for measuring lengths, areas, or volumes.

Information Overlays and Data Visualization

AR can enhance your perception of the world by overlaying information and visualizing data in real-time, providing context and insights that would otherwise be hidden.

Information Overlays

AR can provide contextual information about objects or locations by overlaying text, images, or videos on the camera view. This can enrich your understanding of the world around you and provide access to relevant information at a glance.

- Applications:
    - Object Recognition and Labeling: Identify objects in the environment and overlay labels with their names or descriptions.
    - Historical Information: Overlay historical facts or images on landmarks or historical sites.
    - Product Information: Scan product barcodes or QR codes to overlay information about the product, such as reviews, prices, or specifications.

○ Real-time Translations: Translate text in real-time by pointing the camera at signs or documents.

Data Visualization

AR can bring data to life by visualizing it in 3D space, providing a more intuitive and engaging way to understand complex information. This can involve:

- 3D Charts and Graphs: Display charts and graphs as 3D objects in the AR scene, allowing users to interact with them and explore data from different angles.
- Data-Driven Animations: Create animations that are driven by real-time data, such as visualizing weather patterns or traffic flow.
- Spatial Data Visualization: Overlay data on maps or 3D models of environments, such as visualizing pollution levels or population density.

Example: AR City Guide

Imagine an AR city guide that overlays information about points of interest as you explore a city.

- Interaction: Users point their camera at buildings or landmarks to see information overlays.

- Information Display: Overlay text, images, or videos about the point of interest, such as historical facts, opening hours, or reviews.
- Navigation Integration: Integrate with AR navigation features to guide users to points of interest.

Practical AR Tools for Everyday Use

AR has the potential to revolutionize the way we perform everyday tasks, providing us with tools that can simplify our lives, enhance our productivity, and improve our well-being.

Examples of AR Utility Applications

- AR Shopping Assistants: Help users find products in stores, compare prices, or visualize furniture in their homes before purchasing.
- AR Home Maintenance: Provide step-by-step instructions for home maintenance tasks, such as assembling furniture or fixing appliances.
- AR Fitness Trackers: Overlay fitness data and guidance during workouts, providing motivation and feedback.
- AR Language Learning: Overlay translations or pronunciation guides in real-time to assist with language learning.

- AR Accessibility Tools: Assist people with disabilities by providing visual or auditory cues, real-time object recognition, or navigation assistance.

Designing for Usability

When building AR utility applications, focus on usability and practicality. The AR features should be intuitive, easy to use, and seamlessly integrated into the user's workflow.

- Clear UI: Design a clear and uncluttered user interface that doesn't obstruct the AR view.
- Intuitive Interactions: Use natural and intuitive interaction methods, such as touch gestures or voice commands.
- Contextual Information: Provide relevant information at the right time and place, avoiding information overload.
- Performance: Ensure smooth performance and minimal battery consumption.

Example: AR Task Reminder

Imagine an AR application that reminds users of tasks by placing virtual sticky notes on objects or locations in their environment.

- Interaction: Users can create virtual sticky notes by speaking or typing reminders and then attaching them to objects or locations in the AR view.
- Reminders: The application reminds users of tasks when they are near the associated object or location.
- Customization: Allow users to customize the appearance and behavior of the sticky notes, such as colors, sizes, or reminder times.

Code Challenge: AR Home Decorator

Let's create an AR application that helps users visualize furniture and decor in their homes!

Objective: Develop an AR application that allows users to place virtual furniture and decor items in their real-world environment.

Tools: OpenCV, a 3D model library (or 3D modeling tool), camera, plane detection.

Steps:

1. Plane Detection: Detect planar surfaces in the environment, such as floors or tabletops.

2. Object Placement: Allow users to select and place virtual furniture or decor items on the detected planes.
3. Object Manipulation: Allow users to move, rotate, and scale the virtual objects using touch gestures or motion controls.
4. Realistic Rendering: Render the virtual objects with realistic lighting and shadows to enhance the illusion of them being present in the real world.

This challenge will allow you to apply your knowledge of plane detection, object placement, and 3D rendering to create a practical AR tool that can assist with home decorating and design.

Congratulations! You've now explored the world of building AR utility applications. You can create tools for real-time measurement and navigation, overlay information and visualize data, and design practical AR solutions for everyday use. Go forth and use your AR skills to enhance your life and the lives of others!

Part VII: Deployment and Beyond

Chapter 15: Fine-Tuning Your AR Creations: Optimizing AR Applications

Prepare to elevate your AR applications from good to great! In this chapter, we'll delve into the crucial art of optimization, ensuring your creations run smoothly, efficiently, and provide the best possible user experience. We'll explore performance profiling and analysis, master code optimization techniques, and discover strategies for reducing latency and improving frame rates.

By the end, you'll have the knowledge and tools to fine-tune your AR applications, ensuring they perform at their peak on various devices and deliver seamless and immersive experiences. Let's embark on this journey of AR optimization!

Performance Profiling and Analysis

Before we can optimize our AR applications, we need to identify the bottlenecks and areas that need improvement. Performance profiling and analysis are like diagnostic tools that help us understand how our applications are performing and where the performance issues lie.

Why Profile?

Performance profiling helps us:

- Identify Bottlenecks: Pinpoint the specific parts of our code or AR pipeline that are causing performance issues.
- Measure Performance: Quantify the performance of different components and track improvements over time.
- Understand Resource Usage: Analyze how our application utilizes resources like CPU, memory, and GPU.
- Make Informed Decisions: Make data-driven decisions about which optimization techniques to apply.

Profiling Tools

Various profiling tools are available for AR development, including:

- OpenCV Profiler: OpenCV provides built-in profiling tools that can measure the execution time of different functions and code blocks.
- System Profilers: Operating systems like Windows, macOS, and Linux provide system profilers that can analyze CPU usage, memory allocation, and other system-level metrics.

- AR Platform Profilers: AR platforms like ARKit and ARCore often include profiling tools that can analyze performance specific to AR features, such as tracking, rendering, and plane detection.
- External Profilers: Specialized profiling tools like VTune Amplifier or NVIDIA Nsight Graphics can provide deeper insights into performance bottlenecks.

Profiling Techniques

- Timing Code Execution: Measure the execution time of specific functions or code blocks using timers or profiling tools.
- Analyzing CPU Usage: Use system profilers or dedicated CPU profiling tools to identify functions or threads that are consuming excessive CPU resources.
- Memory Profiling: Analyze memory allocation and usage patterns to identify memory leaks or excessive memory consumption.
- GPU Profiling: If your AR application utilizes the GPU for rendering or computer vision tasks, use GPU profiling tools to analyze GPU usage and identify potential bottlenecks.

Analyzing the AR Pipeline

When profiling AR applications, it's important to consider the entire AR pipeline:

- Camera Capture: Analyze the frame rate and resolution of the camera feed.
- Computer Vision: Profile the performance of computer vision tasks like object detection, tracking, and pose estimation.
- Rendering: Analyze the rendering performance, including the number of polygons, draw calls, and shader complexity.
- AR Features: If using AR platform features like plane detection or anchors, profile their performance.

Example: Profiling with OpenCV

Python

```
import cv2

import time


 Start the timer

start_time = time.time()


... (Code to be profiled) ...
```

```
End the timer
end_time = time.time()


Calculate the execution time
execution_time = end_time - start_time


Print the execution time
print(f"Execution time: {execution_time:.4f} seconds")
```

This example demonstrates how to use Python's time module to measure the execution time of a code block. You can use this technique to profile different parts of your AR application and identify potential bottlenecks.

Code Optimization Techniques

Once you've identified performance bottlenecks through profiling, it's time to apply code optimization techniques to improve the efficiency of your AR application.

Algorithm Optimization

Choosing the right algorithms and data structures can significantly impact performance. Consider the following:

- Efficient Algorithms: Select algorithms that are optimized for the specific task and the target hardware.
- Data Structures: Use appropriate data structures that minimize memory usage and access time.
- Complexity Analysis: Analyze the time and space complexity of your algorithms to understand their scalability.

Loop Optimization

Loops are often performance hotspots in AR applications. Optimize them by:

- Minimizing Loop Iterations: Reduce the number of iterations by pre-calculating values or using efficient data structures.
- Loop Unrolling: Manually unroll small loops to reduce loop overhead.
- Vectorization: Use vectorized operations (like NumPy arrays) to perform calculations on multiple data elements simultaneously.

Memory Management

Efficient memory management can prevent memory leaks and improve performance.

- Avoid Memory Leaks: Release resources (like images or memory buffers) when they are no longer needed.
- Memory Pooling: Reuse memory blocks instead of constantly allocating and deallocating memory.
- Data Sharing: Share data between different parts of your application instead of creating duplicate copies.

Code Refactoring

Refactor your code to improve its readability, maintainability, and performance.

- Remove Redundant Code: Eliminate unnecessary calculations or duplicate code.
- Function Inlining: Inline small functions to reduce function call overhead.
- Code Reusability: Create reusable functions or classes to avoid code duplication.

Example: Optimizing a Loop

Python

```
import numpy as np


Original loop
result = []
for i in range(1000):
    result.append(i  2)


Optimized loop with vectorization
result = np.arange(1000)  2
```

This example demonstrates how to optimize a loop using vectorization. The original loop iterates 1000 times, while the optimized version uses a NumPy array to perform the calculation on all elements simultaneously, resulting in a significant performance improvement.

Reducing Latency and Improving Frame Rates

Latency is the delay between an action and its effect. In AR applications, latency can manifest as a lag between the user's movements and the corresponding update in the AR scene. High latency can break the illusion of immersion and cause motion sickness.

Frame rate is the number of frames displayed per second. A higher frame rate results in smoother and more fluid motion in the AR scene.

Causes of Latency

- Camera Capture: The time it takes to capture a frame from the camera.
- Computer Vision: The processing time required for computer vision tasks like object detection and tracking.
- Rendering: The time it takes to render the AR scene.
- Synchronization: The time it takes to synchronize the AR scene with the real-world view.

Techniques for Reducing Latency

- Optimize Camera Capture: Use a higher frame rate camera, reduce the image resolution, or use hardware acceleration for camera capture.
- Optimize Computer Vision: Use efficient computer vision algorithms, reduce the complexity of the tasks, or use hardware acceleration for computer vision processing.

- Optimize Rendering: Reduce the number of polygons, draw calls, and shader complexity. Use techniques like level of detail (LOD) rendering to render objects with varying levels of detail based on their distance from the camera.
- Asynchronous Operations: Perform computationally intensive tasks asynchronously to avoid blocking the main thread and maintain a responsive UI.

Techniques for Improving Frame Rates

- Reduce Rendering Load: Optimize 3D models, reduce the number of objects in the scene, and use efficient rendering techniques.
- Optimize Computer Vision: Use faster computer vision algorithms or reduce the frequency of computer vision processing.
- Multithreading: Utilize multithreading to perform tasks in parallel and improve overall performance.
- Hardware Acceleration: Leverage hardware acceleration for rendering and computer vision tasks.

Example: Asynchronous Operations

Python

```python
import asyncio

async def perform_heavy_task():
    ... (Perform a computationally intensive task) ...

async def main():
    Create a task for the heavy task
    task = asyncio.create_task(perform_heavy_task())

    Continue with other operations while the task is running

    ...

    Wait for the task to complete
    await task

Run the main function
asyncio.run(main())
```

This example demonstrates how to use asynchronous operations in Python to perform a computationally intensive task without blocking the main thread. This can help reduce latency and maintain a responsive UI in your AR application.

Code Challenge: Performance Optimization Challenge

Let's put your optimization skills to the test!

Objective: Take an existing AR application (e.g., one of the previous code challenges) and optimize its performance to achieve a higher frame rate and reduced latency.

Tools: Profiling tools, code optimization techniques, AR platform profilers.

Steps:

1. Performance Profiling: Use profiling tools to identify performance bottlenecks in the application.
2. Code Optimization: Apply code optimization techniques to improve the efficiency of the code.
3. Latency Reduction: Implement techniques to reduce latency and improve responsiveness.
4. Frame Rate Improvement: Optimize rendering and computer vision to achieve a higher frame rate.

5. Performance Testing: Test the optimized application on different devices and compare its performance to the original version.

This challenge will allow you to apply your knowledge of performance profiling, code optimization, and latency reduction to create a more efficient and enjoyable AR experience.

Congratulations! You've now mastered the art of optimizing AR applications. You can profile performance, apply code optimization techniques, and reduce latency to create smooth, efficient, and immersive AR experiences. Keep refining your skills and pushing the boundaries of AR development!

Chapter 16: Sharing Your AR Magic: Deploying AR Applications

Congratulations on creating your amazing AR applications! Now it's time to share your creations with the world. In this chapter, we'll guide you through the process of deploying your AR apps, making them accessible to users on different platforms. We'll explore how to package your apps for various devices, discuss distribution channels, and navigate the exciting world of AR app stores and marketplaces.

By the end, you'll be equipped to bring your AR magic to the masses, allowing users to experience your creations on their smartphones, tablets, and AR glasses. Let's embark on this journey of AR deployment!

Packaging AR Apps for Different Platforms

The world of AR encompasses a variety of platforms and devices, each with its own unique requirements and specifications. To successfully deploy your AR applications, you need to package them correctly for each target platform.

Understanding Platform Differences

- Mobile Platforms (iOS and Android): The dominant platforms for AR experiences, with millions of users accessing AR through their smartphones and tablets.
    - iOS: Requires packaging apps in the .ipa format and distributing them through the Apple App Store.
    - Android: Requires packaging apps in the .apk format and distributing them through the Google Play Store or other Android app stores.
- AR Glasses and Headsets: Dedicated AR devices like Microsoft HoloLens, Magic Leap, and upcoming glasses from companies like Apple offer more immersive and hands-free AR experiences.
    - Platform-Specific SDKs: Each AR glasses platform has its own Software Development Kit (SDK) and packaging requirements.
- WebAR: AR experiences accessible through web browsers, eliminating the need for users to download and install apps.
    - Web Standards: WebAR relies on web standards like WebXR, which allows for cross-platform compatibility.

Packaging Tools and Frameworks

- Unity: A popular game engine that provides cross-platform AR development and deployment tools. You can build AR apps for iOS, Android, and various AR glasses using Unity.
- Unreal Engine: Another powerful game engine with AR development capabilities, offering cross-platform support and advanced rendering features.
- ARKit and ARCore: These platform-specific SDKs provide tools for packaging AR apps for iOS and Android devices, respectively.
- WebXR Libraries: Libraries like A-Frame, Babylon.js, and Three.js can be used to package WebAR experiences.

Packaging Considerations

- Platform Requirements: Ensure your app meets the specific requirements of each target platform, such as screen resolution, hardware capabilities, and operating system versions.
- Performance Optimization: Optimize your app's performance for each platform, considering factors like processing power, memory limitations, and battery consumption.

- User Interface: Adapt your app's user interface to the specific input methods and screen sizes of each platform.
- Testing: Thoroughly test your app on each platform to ensure it functions correctly and provides a positive user experience.

Example: Packaging an AR App with Unity

Conceptual example using Unity

1. Build Settings: In Unity, go to File > Build Settings.

2. Platform Selection: Select the target platform (e.g., iOS, Android).

3. SDK Setup: Ensure the necessary SDKs are installed and configured for the selected platform.

4. Player Settings: Configure player settings specific to the platform, such as app icons, splash screens, and required permissions.

5. Build: Click "Build" to generate the app package for the selected platform.

This example demonstrates the basic steps for packaging an AR app using Unity. The specific settings and options may vary depending on the target platform and the AR features used in your application.

Distributing Your AR App

Once you've packaged your AR app for different platforms, it's time to distribute it to users. There are various distribution channels available, each with its own advantages and considerations.

App Stores

App stores are the primary distribution channels for mobile AR applications.

- Apple App Store: For iOS apps. Requires creating a developer account and submitting your app for review.
- Google Play Store: For Android apps. Also requires a developer account and app review process.
- Other App Stores: Alternative app stores like Amazon Appstore or Samsung Galaxy Store can also be used to distribute your app.

Direct Distribution

You can also distribute your app directly to users, bypassing app stores.

- Website: Host your app on your website and provide download links for different platforms.
- Email: Distribute your app through email campaigns or newsletters.
- Social Media: Share your app on social media platforms and encourage users to download it.

Considerations for Distribution

- Target Audience: Consider your target audience and choose distribution channels that reach them effectively.
- Marketing and Promotion: Promote your app through various channels like social media, online advertising, or press releases.
- User Acquisition: Implement strategies to acquire users, such as offering free trials, discounts, or in-app promotions.
- Analytics and Tracking: Use analytics tools to track app downloads, usage patterns, and user engagement.

Example: Publishing an AR App on the App Store

Conceptual example for the Apple App Store

1. Developer Account: Create an Apple Developer account.

2. App Store Connect: Prepare your app's metadata (title, description, screenshots, etc.) in App Store Connect.

3. Xcode: Use Xcode to archive and upload your app to App Store Connect.

4. App Review: Submit your app for review by Apple.

5. Release: Once approved, release your app on the App Store.

This example demonstrates the general process for publishing an AR app on the Apple App Store. The specific steps and requirements may vary depending on the app's features and content.

AR App Stores and Marketplaces

In addition to general app stores, there are emerging AR-specific app stores and marketplaces that focus on showcasing and distributing AR experiences.

AR-Focused Platforms

- VRChat: A social VR platform that also supports AR experiences, allowing users to create and share avatars, worlds, and games.

- Spatial: A platform for collaborative AR experiences, enabling users to create shared workspaces, presentations, and events.
- Snap Lens Network: A platform for creating and sharing AR lenses for Snapchat, offering a wide reach and creative tools.
- 8th Wall: A platform for developing and distributing WebAR experiences, providing tools for creating immersive and interactive AR content without the need for app downloads.

Benefits of AR Marketplaces

- Targeted Audience: AR marketplaces attract users who are specifically interested in AR experiences, increasing the visibility of your app.
- Community and Collaboration: AR marketplaces often foster a sense of community and collaboration among developers and users.
- Discovery and Promotion: AR marketplaces can help users discover your app and provide opportunities for promotion.
- Monetization: Some AR marketplaces offer monetization options, allowing you to earn revenue from your app.

Example: Publishing an AR Lens on Snapchat

Conceptual example for Snap Lens Network

1. Lens Studio: Create your AR lens using Snap's Lens Studio tool.

2. Lens Network: Submit your lens to the Snap Lens Network for review.

3. Publishing: Once approved, your lens will be published and discoverable by Snapchat users.

This example demonstrates the general process for publishing an AR lens on Snapchat. The specific steps and requirements may vary depending on the lens's complexity and features.

Code Challenge: Deploying Your AR Game

Let's take one of your AR games and deploy it to a mobile platform!

Objective: Choose an AR game you've developed (e.g., from a previous code challenge) and package it for either iOS or Android. Distribute the app through an app store or direct distribution channel.

Tools: Unity, ARKit (for iOS) or ARCore (for Android), Xcode (for iOS), Android Studio (for Android).

Steps:

1. Platform Choice: Choose the target platform (iOS or Android).
2. Packaging: Use Unity or the platform-specific SDKs to package your game for the chosen platform.
3. Distribution: Distribute your game through an app store (Apple App Store or Google Play Store) or a direct distribution channel (website, email, social media).
4. Testing: Thoroughly test your game on the target platform to ensure it functions correctly and provides a positive user experience.

This challenge will allow you to experience the full cycle of AR development, from concept to deployment, and share your AR creation with the world.

Congratulations! You've now learned the essential elements of deploying AR applications. You can package your apps for different platforms, distribute them through various channels, and navigate the world of AR app stores and marketplaces. Go forth and share your AR magic with the world!

Chapter 17: Gazing into the Crystal Ball: The Future of AR Development

Prepare to step beyond the present and explore the exciting possibilities that lie ahead for Augmented Reality! In this chapter, we'll delve into the emerging technologies and trends shaping the future of AR, examine the transformative potential of WebAR and cloud-based AR, and grapple with the ethical considerations that will guide responsible AR development.

By the end, you'll have a glimpse into the future of AR, gaining insights into the technologies, platforms, and ethical frameworks that will shape the next generation of immersive experiences. Let's embark on this journey into the future of AR!

Emerging AR Technologies and Trends

The world of AR is constantly evolving, with new technologies and trends emerging at a rapid pace. These advancements promise to make AR experiences more immersive, accessible, and seamlessly integrated with our lives.

Hardware Advancements

- AR Glasses and Headsets: AR glasses are becoming lighter, more comfortable, and more powerful, with improved displays, sensors, and processing capabilities. Companies like Apple, Google, and Meta are investing heavily in AR glasses, promising to revolutionize how we interact with the digital world.
  - Waveguide Displays: These advanced displays offer wider fields of view, higher resolution, and better transparency, creating more immersive and realistic AR experiences.
  - Eye Tracking and Hand Tracking: These technologies allow for more natural and intuitive interactions with AR content, enabling users to control virtual objects with their gaze or hand gestures.
  - Spatial Audio: Creates realistic 3D soundscapes that enhance immersion and provide directional cues in AR experiences.
- Mobile Devices: Smartphones and tablets continue to be the primary platforms for AR experiences, with advancements in camera technology, processing power, and sensor capabilities driving innovation in mobile AR.

- Depth Sensing: Improved depth sensing technologies like LiDAR enable more accurate environment understanding and object placement in AR applications.
- AI Chips: Dedicated AI chips on mobile devices accelerate machine learning tasks like object recognition and pose estimation, enabling more intelligent and responsive AR experiences.

Software and Platform Innovations

- AR Cloud: The AR Cloud is a shared, persistent 3D map of the world that enables collaborative and persistent AR experiences. It allows users to interact with virtual content anchored to real-world locations and share those experiences with others.
  - Persistent AR: Virtual objects can persist in the AR Cloud, remaining in the same location even when users leave and return to the area.
  - Shared AR: Multiple users can interact with the same virtual content in the AR Cloud, enabling collaborative experiences and shared virtual worlds.

- Artificial Intelligence (AI): AI plays an increasingly crucial role in AR, enabling more intelligent and personalized experiences.
  - Scene Understanding: AI algorithms can analyze the environment, recognize objects, and understand context, allowing AR applications to adapt to the user's surroundings.
  - Personalized Content: AI can personalize AR experiences based on user preferences, behavior, and context.
  - Natural Interactions: AI enables more natural and intuitive interactions with AR content, such as voice commands, gesture recognition, and eye tracking.
- 5G and Edge Computing: Faster and more reliable connectivity with 5G and edge computing will enable more complex and data-intensive AR applications.
  - Real-time Streaming: Stream high-quality 3D content and experiences in real-time, reducing latency and improving immersion.
  - Cloud-based Processing: Offload computationally intensive tasks to the cloud, enabling more complex AR experiences on resource-constrained devices.

Example: AR Collaboration with Spatial

Imagine a collaborative AR workspace where colleagues can interact with shared virtual objects and data, even when they are physically located in different parts of the world. Spatial is a platform that enables such experiences, allowing users to create shared AR workspaces, presentations, and events.

WebAR and Cloud-based AR

WebAR and cloud-based AR are transforming the accessibility and scalability of AR experiences, making them easier to create, share, and access on a wider range of devices.

WebAR

WebAR allows users to experience AR directly through their web browsers, without the need to download and install dedicated apps. This significantly lowers the barrier to entry for AR, making it more accessible to a wider audience.

- WebXR: WebXR is a web standard that provides an API for creating immersive web experiences, including AR and VR. It allows developers to access device capabilities like cameras, sensors, and displays to create cross-platform AR experiences.

- Benefits of WebAR:
  - Accessibility: Users can access WebAR experiences on a wide range of devices, including smartphones, tablets, and desktops, without the need for app downloads.
  - Ease of Sharing: WebAR experiences can be easily shared through links or embedded in web pages, making them readily accessible.
  - Cost-Effectiveness: WebAR development can be more cost-effective than native app development, as it eliminates the need for platform-specific SDKs and app store submissions.

Cloud-based AR

Cloud-based AR leverages the power of cloud computing to enhance AR experiences, enabling more complex and data-intensive applications.

- Benefits of Cloud-based AR:
  - Scalability: Cloud-based AR can handle large numbers of users and complex AR scenes, as the processing is offloaded to powerful cloud servers.

- Reduced Device Requirements: Cloud-based AR can enable complex AR experiences on resource-constrained devices, as the heavy lifting is done in the cloud.
- Persistent and Shared Experiences: The AR Cloud enables persistent and shared AR experiences, where virtual content is anchored to real-world locations and can be accessed by multiple users.

Example: WebAR Product Visualization

Imagine a furniture retailer offering a WebAR experience on their website that allows users to visualize furniture in their homes before purchasing. Users can simply visit the website on their smartphone or tablet, point their camera at their living room, and place virtual furniture items in the scene to see how they look and fit.

Ethical Considerations in AR

As AR becomes more prevalent and integrated with our lives, it's crucial to consider the ethical implications and ensure that this powerful technology is used responsibly.

Privacy and Data Security

AR applications often collect personal data, such as location, facial features, and even eye movements. It's essential to protect this data and ensure that it's used ethically and responsibly.

- Data Minimization: Collect only the data that is absolutely necessary for the AR experience.
- Informed Consent: Obtain explicit consent from users before collecting or using their data.
- Data Security: Implement robust security measures to protect user data from unauthorized access or misuse.
- Transparency: Be transparent with users about how their data is being collected, used, and stored.

Misinformation and Manipulation

AR has the potential to blur the lines between reality and virtuality, raising concerns about misinformation and manipulation.

- Authenticity and Trust: Ensure that AR experiences are clearly distinguishable from reality and do not deceive users.
- Content Moderation: Implement measures to prevent the spread of misinformation or harmful content through AR applications.

- Responsible Design: Design AR experiences that promote critical thinking and media literacy.

Accessibility and Inclusivity

AR experiences should be designed to be accessible to everyone, including people with disabilities.

- Inclusive Design: Consider the needs of users with diverse abilities and ensure that AR experiences are accessible to them.
- Assistive Technologies: Integrate AR with assistive technologies to enhance accessibility for people with disabilities.

Social and Cultural Impact

AR has the potential to significantly impact social norms, cultural values, and human behavior.

- Social Responsibility: Consider the potential social and cultural impact of AR experiences and design them to promote positive outcomes.
- Digital Divide: Address the digital divide and ensure that AR technology is accessible to all communities.

Example: Responsible AR Advertising

Imagine an AR advertising campaign that overlays virtual billboards on real-world buildings. It's crucial to ensure that these virtual billboards are clearly distinguishable from real signage and do not mislead or confuse users. The campaign should also respect user privacy and avoid collecting unnecessary data.

Code Challenge: Ethical AR Design Challenge

Let's explore ethical considerations in AR development through a design challenge!

Objective: Choose an AR application idea (e.g., a social AR experience, an AR game, or an AR utility tool) and design it with ethical considerations in mind.

Steps:

1. Identify Ethical Concerns: Identify potential ethical concerns related to your AR application idea, such as privacy, misinformation, accessibility, or social impact.
2. Design for Ethics: Design your AR application to address these ethical concerns, incorporating features or design choices that promote responsible AR development.
3. Ethical Framework: Develop an ethical framework for your AR application, outlining the

principles and guidelines that will guide its development and use.

This challenge will encourage you to think critically about the ethical implications of AR and design AR experiences that are responsible, inclusive, and beneficial to society.

Congratulations! You've now explored the future of AR development, gaining insights into emerging technologies, WebAR, cloud-based AR, and ethical considerations. As you continue your AR journey, remember to embrace innovation, prioritize user experience, and contribute to the responsible development of this transformative technology. The future of AR is bright, and with your skills and creativity, you can help shape it into a positive force for change.

Conclusion: Stepping into the Future of Augmented Reality

As you reach the end of this journey through the world of Augmented Reality development with Python and OpenCV, we hope you feel empowered to create your own magical AR experiences. We've covered a vast landscape, from the fundamental concepts of AR to advanced techniques like 3D reconstruction, machine learning integration, and performance optimization.

You've learned to harness the power of OpenCV to manipulate images, detect objects, track markers, and understand the environment. You've delved into the intricacies of 3D graphics, rendering virtual objects that seamlessly blend with the real world. You've even explored the ethical considerations that will guide the responsible development of AR technologies.

But this is just the beginning. The field of AR is constantly evolving, with new technologies and possibilities emerging every day. AR glasses are on the horizon, promising to revolutionize how we interact with the digital world. The AR Cloud is taking shape, enabling persistent and shared AR experiences. Artificial intelligence is infusing AR with intelligence and personalization.

As you continue your AR journey, remember to:

- Embrace Innovation: Stay curious and explore the latest AR technologies and trends. Experiment with new tools, libraries, and platforms.
- Prioritize User Experience: Design AR experiences that are intuitive, engaging, and user-friendly. Consider the needs of your users and strive to create experiences that are accessible and inclusive.
- Develop Responsibly: Be mindful of the ethical implications of AR and contribute to the responsible development of this powerful technology.

The future of AR is filled with exciting possibilities. With your newfound skills and creativity, you can be a part of this transformative journey, creating AR experiences that entertain, educate, and enhance our lives. Go forth and unleash your AR magic!

Key Takeaways:

- AR is a powerful technology with the potential to revolutionize various industries and aspects of our lives.

- Python and OpenCV provide a versatile and accessible toolkit for AR development.
- Mastering the fundamentals of computer vision, 3D graphics, and AR techniques is essential for creating compelling AR experiences.
- Continuous learning and exploration are crucial for staying at the forefront of AR innovation.
- Ethical considerations should guide the development and deployment of AR applications.

We hope this book has provided you with a solid foundation in AR development and inspired you to create your own AR magic. Now go out there and build the future of Augmented Reality!

Appendix

This appendix provides valuable resources and information to further assist you on your AR development journey. It includes troubleshooting tips for common AR development issues, a curated list of resources for further learning, and a concise OpenCV API reference for quick access to essential functions.

Troubleshooting Common AR Development Issues

AR development can be challenging, and you may encounter various issues along the way. This section provides troubleshooting tips and solutions for some common problems you might face.

Marker Detection Problems

- Markers Not Detected:
    - Poor Lighting: Ensure adequate lighting conditions. Avoid harsh shadows or glare that can obscure the markers.
    - Marker Quality: Make sure the markers are printed or displayed clearly with good contrast.

- Camera Focus: Ensure the camera is properly focused on the markers.
- Camera Distortion: Calibrate the camera to correct for lens distortion.
- Marker Size and Distance: The marker size and distance from the camera should be appropriate for the detection algorithm.
- Inaccurate Pose Estimation:
  - Camera Calibration: Ensure accurate camera calibration.
  - Marker Occlusion: Avoid occluding (blocking) the markers from the camera's view.
  - Marker Movement: Rapid marker movement can affect pose estimation accuracy.

3D Rendering Issues

- Objects Not Displayed:
  - Pose Estimation: Verify that the pose estimation is accurate.
  - Object Visibility: Ensure the object is within the camera's view frustum and not hidden behind other objects.
  - Rendering Code: Check for errors in the rendering code.
- Objects Flickering or Jittering:

- Tracking Stability: Improve marker tracking or feature tracking stability.
- Rendering Performance: Optimize rendering performance to ensure smooth frame rates.

Performance Issues

- Low Frame Rates:
  - Code Optimization: Optimize code for efficiency, reduce unnecessary calculations, and use appropriate data structures.
  - Rendering Optimization: Reduce polygon count, use level of detail (LOD) rendering, and optimize shaders.
  - Computer Vision Optimization: Use efficient computer vision algorithms and consider hardware acceleration.
- High Latency:
  - Asynchronous Operations: Perform computationally intensive tasks asynchronously.
  - Camera Capture: Use a higher frame rate camera or reduce image resolution.
  - Synchronization: Optimize synchronization between the AR scene and the real-world view.

Platform-Specific Issues

- iOS:
    - ARKit Compatibility: Ensure your device and iOS version are compatible with ARKit.
    - Code Signing: Properly code sign your app for distribution.
    - Permissions: Request necessary permissions (e.g., camera access) in your app's Info.plist file.
- Android:
    - ARCore Compatibility: Ensure your device and Android version are compatible with ARCore.
    - Manifest Configuration: Configure your app's AndroidManifest.xml file with necessary permissions and features.
    - Dependencies: Include required ARCore dependencies in your project.

General Troubleshooting Tips

- Check for Errors: Carefully examine error messages and logs to identify the source of the problem.
- Simplify the Scene: Start with a simple AR scene and gradually add complexity to isolate issues.

- Online Resources: Search for solutions online, consult forums, or ask for help from the AR development community.
- Debugging Tools: Use debugging tools to step through your code and identify errors.
- Version Control: Use version control systems like Git to track changes and revert to previous versions if necessary.

Resources and Further Reading

This section provides a curated list of resources to deepen your understanding of AR development and explore advanced topics.

Books

- Mastering OpenCV 4: A comprehensive guide to OpenCV, covering various computer vision techniques and applications.
- Multiple View Geometry in Computer Vision: A classic textbook on the geometry of multiple views, essential for understanding 3D reconstruction techniques.
- Augmented Reality: Principles and Practice: A comprehensive overview of AR principles, technologies, and applications.

Online Courses and Tutorials

- OpenCV Tutorials: Official OpenCV tutorials covering various computer vision topics.
- PyImageSearch: A website with in-depth tutorials and articles on computer vision and deep learning with Python.
- Coursera and edX: Online learning platforms offering courses on AR development, computer vision, and machine learning.

AR Development Platforms and SDKs

- ARKit (Apple): AR development platform for iOS devices.
- ARCore (Google): AR development platform for Android devices.
- Vuforia: A popular AR development platform with cross-platform support.
- Wikitude: Another cross-platform AR development platform with a focus on location-based AR.

Research Papers and Articles

- ARXIV: A repository of research papers on various topics, including computer vision and AR.

- IEEE Xplore: A digital library with a vast collection of research articles on AR and related technologies.

Communities and Forums

- OpenCV Forum: A forum for discussing OpenCV-related topics and seeking help from the community.
- Reddit: Subreddits like r/AR_MR_XR and r/computervision provide a platform for discussions and sharing resources.
- Stack Overflow: A question-and-answer website where you can find solutions to common AR development problems.

OpenCV API Reference

This section provides a concise reference for some commonly used OpenCV functions in AR development.

Image Processing

- cv2.imread(filename): Reads an image from a file.
- cv2.imshow(winname, mat): Displays an image in a window.
- cv2.cvtColor(src, code): Converts an image from one color space to another.

- cv2.resize(src, dsize[, fx[, fy[, interpolation]]]): Resizes an image.
- cv2.GaussianBlur(src, ksize, sigmaX[, sigmaY[, borderType]]]): Applies Gaussian blurring to an image.
- cv2.Canny(image, threshold1, threshold2[, edges[, apertureSize[, L2gradient]]]): Detects edges in an image using the Canny algorithm.

Video Processing

- cv2.VideoCapture(index): Opens a video capture device (e.g., camera).
- cap.read(): Reads a frame from the video capture device.
- cv2.absdiff(src1, src2): Calculates the absolute difference between two images.
- cv2.calcOpticalFlowPyrLK(prevImg, nextImg, prevPts, nextPts[, status[, err[, winSize[, maxLevel[, criteria[, flags[, minEigThreshold]]]]]]]): Calculates optical flow using the Lucas-Kanade method.

Feature Detection and Matching

- cv2.goodFeaturesToTrack(image, maxCorners, qualityLevel, minDistance[, corners[, mask[, blockSize[, useHarrisDetector[, k]]]]]): Detects corners in an image using the Shi-Tomasi corner detector.

- cv2.ORB_create([nfeatures[, scaleFactor[, nlevels[, edgeThreshold[, firstLevel[, WTA_K[, scoreType[, patchSize[, fastThreshold]]]]]]]]]): Creates an ORB feature detector.
- orb.detectAndCompute(image, mask): Detects keypoints and computes descriptors using the ORB detector.
- cv2.BFMatcher_create([normType[, crossCheck]]]): Creates a Brute-Force matcher object.
- bf.match(des1, des2): Matches descriptors between two images.

Marker Detection and Pose Estimation

- cv2.aruco.Dictionary_get(dictionary): Retrieves a predefined Aruco dictionary.
- cv2.aruco.detectMarkers(image, dictionary[, corners[, ids[, rejectedImgPoints[, parameters]]]]): Detects Aruco markers in an image.
- cv2.solvePnP(objectPoints, imagePoints, cameraMatrix, distCoeffs[, rvec[, tvec[, useExtrinsicGuess[, flags]]]]): Estimates the pose of a 3D object from 2D image points.

3D Reconstruction

- cv2.triangulatePoints(projMatr1, projMatr2, projPoints1, projPoints2): Reconstructs 3D points from two sets of 2D projections.

This API reference provides a quick overview of some essential OpenCV functions. For a complete and detailed API reference, refer to the official OpenCV documentation.

Index

- Structure and advantages
- Detection with OpenCV (apriltag library)
- Applications in AR
  - AR applications
    - AR games (examples: Pokémon Go, Ingress Prime)
    - Educational AR experiences
    - Healthcare applications
    - Industrial applications
    - Retail and e-commerce applications
    - Navigation and wayfinding applications
  - ARCore (Google's AR platform)
    - Plane detection with ARCore
    - Integrating ARCore with OpenCV
    - Deploying AR apps on Android with ARCore
  - ARKit (Apple's AR platform)
    - Plane detection with ARKit
    - Integrating ARKit with OpenCV
    - Deploying AR apps on iOS with ARKit
  - AR markers
    - Types of markers (Aruco, AprilTag, QR codes)
    - Characteristics of good markers

- Camera pose estimation
  - Using cv2.solvePnP()
  - Applications in AR (object placement, 3D tracking)
- Canny edge detector (cv2.Canny())
- Collision detection
  - Techniques (bounding boxes, ray casting)
  - Applications in AR games and simulations
- Color spaces
  - BGR, grayscale, HSV
  - Converting between color spaces (cv2.cvtColor())
  - Applications in AR (color tracking, object segmentation)
- Computer vision
  - Fundamentals of computer vision
  - OpenCV library for computer vision
  - Applications in AR
- Contours
  - Finding contours in images (cv2.findContours())
  - Applications in AR (object detection, shape analysis)

- D
  - Data visualization in AR

- Plane detection
- Depth estimation
- SLAM
- Applications in AR (object placement, interaction, navigation)
  - Ethical considerations in AR
    - Privacy and data security
    - Misinformation and manipulation
    - Accessibility and inclusivity
    - Social and cultural impact

- F

  - Face detection
    - Viola-Jones face detector (cv2.CascadeClassifier())
    - Deep learning-based face detection
  - Face mesh (MediaPipe Face Mesh)
  - Face recognition
    - Applications in AR (security, personalization)
  - Face swapping
    - Techniques and applications in AR
  - Facial expression analysis
    - Applications in AR (emotionally responsive experiences)
  - Facial landmark detection

- MediaPipe Face Mesh for landmark detection
- Applications in AR (face tracking, expression analysis)
  - Feature detection and matching
    - Algorithms (SIFT, SURF, ORB)
    - Applications in AR (object recognition, image stitching, 3D reconstruction)
  - Feature tracking
    - Optical flow (cv2.calcOpticalFlowPyrLK())
    - KLT tracker
    - Applications in AR (markerless tracking, SLAM)
  - Filtering
    - Image filtering techniques (blurring, sharpening, edge detection)
    - Point cloud filtering with Open3D
  - Frame differencing
    - Technique for motion detection
    - Applications in AR
  - Frame rates
    - Factors affecting frame rates
    - Techniques for improving frame rates
- G

- Ambient light, directional light, point light, spot light
  - Loop closure in SLAM
    - Recognizing previously visited locations
  - Loop optimization
    - Techniques for optimizing loops (minimizing iterations, unrolling, vectorization)
- M
  - Machine learning in AR
    - Object detection and recognition (YOLO, TensorFlow)
    - Pose estimation (MediaPipe)
    - Building AI-powered AR experiences
  - Marker detection
    - Aruco marker detection
    - AprilTag marker detection
    - QR code detection
  - Marker-based AR
    - Advantages and disadvantages
    - Applications of marker-based AR
  - Markerless AR
    - Advantages and disadvantages
    - Applications of markerless AR
  - Matplotlib

- ■ Using blurring filters
  - ○ NumPy
    - ■ Using NumPy for image representation and manipulation in AR
- ○
  - ○ Object detection and recognition
    - ■ YOLO algorithm
    - ■ TensorFlow for object detection
    - ■ Integrating object detection with AR
  - ○ Object placement in AR
    - ■ Aligning virtual objects with markers or planes
  - ○ Object tracking
    - ■ MeanShift and CAMShift algorithms
    - ■ Applications in AR (interactive games, object interaction)
  - ○ Occlusion handling in AR
    - ■ Techniques for dealing with marker occlusion
  - ○ OpenCV (Open Source Computer Vision Library)
    - ■ Introduction to OpenCV
    - ■ Installing OpenCV with Python
    - ■ OpenCV API reference
    - ■ Applications in AR

- Open3D
    - Point cloud processing with Open3D
    - Visualization, filtering, segmentation, registration
- Optical flow
    - Lucas-Kanade and Farneback algorithms
    - Applications in AR (feature tracking, motion estimation)
- Optimization techniques
    - Algorithm optimization
    - Loop optimization
    - Memory management
    - Code refactoring
- ORB feature detector
    - cv2.ORB_create()
- P
    - Packaging AR applications
        - Packaging for different platforms (iOS, Android, AR glasses)
        - Tools and frameworks (Unity, Unreal Engine, ARKit, ARCore)
    - Performance optimization
        - Profiling and analysis
        - Code optimization techniques
        - Reducing latency and improving frame rates

- Perspective-n-Point (PnP) algorithm
  - cv2.solvePnP()
  - Applications in AR (pose estimation, object placement)
- Physics engines
  - Bullet, PhysX
  - Integrating physics engines with AR
  - Simulating physics interactions (gravity, collisions, friction)
- Plane detection
  - ARKit and ARCore for plane detection
  - Integrating plane detection with OpenCV
  - Applications in AR (object placement, environment interaction)
- Point cloud processing
  - Open3D library for point cloud processing
  - Visualization, filtering, segmentation, registration
- Point clouds
  - Generating point clouds with stereo vision or SfM
- Pose estimation
  - From markers (cv2.solvePnP())

- Books, online courses, tutorials, platforms, SDKs, research papers, communities
  - Rotation of images (cv2.getRotationMatrix2D(), cv2.warpAffine())
- S
  - Scene understanding in AR
    - Plane detection, depth estimation, object recognition
  - SciPy
    - Using SciPy for image processing and scientific computing in AR
  - Segmentation
    - Image segmentation (thresholding, color tracking)
    - Point cloud segmentation with Open3D
  - Sensors in AR
    - Cameras, depth sensors, accelerometers, gyroscopes, GPS
  - Sensor fusion
    - Combining data from multiple sensors to improve accuracy
  - Sharpening filters
    - Applications in AR (image enhancement)
  - SIFT feature detector

- Simultaneous Localization and Mapping (SLAM)
    - Introduction to SLAM
    - Key components of SLAM
    - Types of SLAM (visual SLAM, lidar SLAM)
    - Building a simple SLAM system with OpenCV
    - Applications in AR (navigation, environment mapping)
- Social AR experiences
    - Designing collaborative and shared AR experiences
- Spatial audio
    - Creating realistic 3D soundscapes in AR
- Spatial computing
    - Convergence of AR, VR, and AI
- Stereo vision
    - Depth estimation with stereo vision
    - OpenCV for stereo vision
- Structure from Motion (SfM)
    - Reconstructing 3D scenes from images
    - OpenMVG and OpenMVS libraries for SfM
- Superimposition-based AR

- V (continued)
  - Video processing
    - Accessing camera feeds with OpenCV (cv2.VideoCapture())
    - Capturing frames from video streams
    - Working with video files
    - Video processing techniques (frame differencing, optical flow, color tracking)
    - Applications in AR (object tracking, motion analysis)
  - Virtual buttons in AR
    - Creating interactive AR interfaces with virtual buttons
  - Virtual Reality (VR)
    - Distinguishing VR from AR
    - The relationship between VR and AR
  - Virtual try-on
    - Applications in AR (retail, fashion)

- Implementing virtual try-on with OpenCV and face tracking
  - Visual SLAM
    - Using cameras for SLAM
    - Applications in AR (navigation, environment mapping)
  - Visualization
    - 3D visualization in AR (educational applications, data visualization)
    - Point cloud visualization with Open3D
  - VS Code IDE
    - Using VS Code for AR development with Python
  - Vuforia AR platform
    - Features and capabilities of Vuforia
    - Integrating Vuforia with OpenCV
- W
  - WebAR
    - AR experiences accessible through web browsers
    - WebXR standard for WebAR development
    - Benefits of WebAR (accessibility, ease of sharing, cost-effectiveness)

www.ingramcontent.com/pod-product-compliance
Lightning Source LLC
La Vergne TN
LVHW022335060326
832902LV00022B/4060